CREATIVE ENDINGS

DESIGNER DYING &
CELEBRATORY FUNERALS

EDITED BY
NICHOLAS ALBERY
LINDESAY IRVINE
PHILIP BUCKLEY
& STEPHANIE PIEAU

COVER ILLUSTRATION BY
ANTHONY COLBERT

Published September 1996 by

The Natural Death Centre
20 Heber Road
London NW2 6AA
tel 0181 208 2853
fax 0181 452 6434
e-mail: <rhino@dial.pipex.com>

Further copies of this book are available from The Natural Death Centre for £5-95 incl. p&p. For a full *Information Pack* about the Centre please send six first class stamps (or a £1-56 cheque). Also available: *The Natural Death Handbook* (to which the present book is a supplement), £10-95 incl. p&p; *Before & After* (the 1995 supplement), £5-95 incl. p&p; *Green Burial – the D-i-y Guide to Law and Practice*, £9-85 incl. p&p.

Copyright © The Natural Death Centre 1996
Resurgence magazine kindly gave permission for use of the cover drawing

The Natural Death Centre is a charity which supports those who are dying at home and provides information to those trying to organise funerals with or without the help of funeral directors. It also works more generally to help improve the quality of dying, through research, awards, publications, meetings, salons and an annual English Day of the Dead in April.

The Natural Death Centre has set up two subsidiary organisations, The Association of Nature Reserve Burial Grounds, which promotes the Green burial grounds set up by councils, farmers and wildlife trusts; and the Befriending Network, which provides volunteers to visit those who are critically ill at home. The Centre has many publications available free on the Internet, at the location:
<http://www.newciv.org/worldtrans/naturaldeath.html>

British Library Cataloguing-in-Publication Data. A catalogue record for this book is available from the British Library.
ISBN 0 9523280 2 X
Printed by Antony Rowe Ltd, Chippenham, Wilts SN14 6QA

Contents

* = Award Winner

Natural Death Centre Awards 1996 5

The Natural Death Centre
1996 – an exhausting year 6

Preparing for dying
What does someone dying need? 7
Rex Winsbury 7
* Joy within the crevices of cancer and fear 12
A commitment to keeping sex alive 13
The limitations of positive thinking 15
Homesharers 18
Keep family informed every 15 minutes 18
Whisper goodbye 19
Hospital cleaners to care for terminally ill 19
A hundred pages of forms for your last wishes 19
'Being with dying' – model projects 20
Joan Halifax 20
Designer dying, Leary-style 23
The drugs that eased Leary's dying days 24
Do people die as they've lived? 24
The good death 26
Sasha's funeral 27
The force of social gravity 27
The individualist's right to be in control 28
Actors without parts to play 28
'Comeditation' – exhaling together with sounds 29
* Fasting to a "comfortable death" 30
Isn't starving to death cruel? 34
Australian territory legalises euthanasia 35
Death awareness leads to moral extremism 36
Michael Kearl 36
American murder statistics 36
How to avoid misdiagnosing death 37
Lower life insurance for agreeing to sell one's organs ... 37
Robin Hanson 37

After death
The Dead Citizens Charter 38
Funeral directors still failing to obey their own code 42

4 Creative Endings

Funeral company's high pressure tactics 42
Common misconceptions within the funeral trade 43
The greening of a cemetery 46
Ken West *46*
Death – a return to the sacred grove 48
Erik van Lennep *48*
The newest green burial grounds 51
The latest on planning permission for d-i-y burials 52
Burial in a Connemara blanket 52
Margaret Love *52*
A family-organised funeral 54
Judith Furner *54*
The dead good funeral 57
A dozen ways to improve funeral arrangements 57
Hanging the crem with banners and papercuts 60
Funeral rituals inspired by the Maoris 61
Funeral balloons threaten turtles 62
Ann Hunt *62*
Tribal funeral practices around the world 63
* A Celebration Box at the back of the church 65
Yvonne Malik *66*
A tombstone with flat-screen video 67
Joey Shamel *67*
Neo-classical ceramic memorial urns 67
Distributing ashes to Poste Restantes 67
Anthony Judge *67*
Make your own video message memorial 68
Obituaries for the ordinary 69
Memorial services for the living 69
Making love in the afterlife 69
Virtual immortality for everyone alive today 70
Professor John Wren-Lewis *70*

LETTERS

Canal boat cruises during terminal illness 73
James B. Marshall *73*
Messages written on papier maché coffins 74
Pamela Gray *74*
Centre for Living and Dying in the States 74
Cliff Aguirre *74*
Practising for dying 75
Thom Osborn *75*
Seeing and touching the dead body 75
Stephen Briggs *75*
A recognised sign to indicate bereavement 76

Creative Endings, £5-95 by credit card from The Natural Death Centre, tel London 0181 208 2853

Natural Death Centre Awards 1996

The Natural Death Centre International Awards 1996 for the most helpful and innovative projects, announced in London on September 1st 1996, go to the following three winners:

• **Yvonne Malik**, a designer living in Wray, Lancashire, UK, is the main £500 Award winner, for her inventiveness and artistry on the theme of death and dying, particularly for her beautiful decorated coffins for adults and children, for her meditation glass panels and for her current proposals for a flat pack, cardboard Celebration Box. This Celebration Box could be placed at the back of the church or crematorium or memorial service, or filled before death, as a kind of miniature art gallery, with photographs, letters, poems, keepsakes and small items. "This is a new way", writes Malik, "of including family and friends in a non-verbal act of celebration – as a later comfort for the bereaved, as well as something to be treasured by the next generation." Malik seeks a sponsor to manufacture and distribute the Celebration Box. See page 65.

• *Fine Black Lines* by Lois Tschetter Hjelmstad (published by the Mulberry Hill Press in Colorado) wins the Natural Death Centre's Best Book Award. In this self-published book, Hjelmstad reviews her experiences of breast cancer, double mastectomy and other ordeals. She distils her insights in fine poetry and with tips for fellow sufferers and those they live with. Themes tackled include a commitment to keeping sex alive (and how the need for intimacy can be misunderstood: "I'm thinking about death – and you're thinking about sex?") and the limitations of positive thinking (which can become an "additional burden", a barrier against talking about what one is really thinking and feeling – "afraid to even mention the possibility of not getting well, as though that would be a jinx"). See page 12.

• **Chris Docker**, of the Voluntary Euthanasia Society of Scotland, wins a Natural Death Centre Award for his excellently-researched 28-page paper on 'The art and science of fasting – Abstinence from food and drink as a means of accelerating death'. Docker points out that fasting is the *only* method at the present time "in which all sides in the 'right to die' debate may reach common agreement under the law"; and quotes research to the effect that fasting is a reassuringly peaceful death, with a further correlation between comfort and lack of medical hydration. A survey of hospice nurses found that "82 per cent disagreed with the statement that dehydration is painful". Docker also describes the Jaina religious group in India, where voluntary fasts to death by those approaching their end are considered dignified yogic deaths. See page 30.

The 1996 Awards were determined by the directors of The Natural Death Centre and its parent body, the Institute for Social Inventions, from their selection of material sent in by correspondents around the world (although winning schemes had to have some applicability to the UK).

Members of the public are invited to nominate possible future winners.

THE NATURAL DEATH CENTRE
1996 – an exhausting year
Nicholas Albery

The year to July '96 has been an exhausting one for the Natural Death Centre, mainly providing advice on funerals by phone and by letter. Besides numerous phone calls every day, there are between 200 and 1,000 letters a week to answer.

The Centre's other projects include:

The Befriending Network, where volunteers visit the homes of those who have a life-threatening illness. The person who is ill, or the family, or any organisation involved, can ask the Befriending Network to make contact, and the volunteer then visits for a couple of hours each week. At present, the Network is still relatively small, based in Oxford and London. More volunteers are urgently needed to join the trainings, which start three times a year. My hope is that more doctors and priests and other neighbourhood opinion leaders will make contact who would like to activate Befriending Networks in their areas – with neighbours urged to help on a rota basis with errands and other assistance for those caring for a person who is dying at home.

The Association of Nature Reserve Burial Grounds continues to grow rapidly. Last year at this time there were 17 woodland burial grounds open. Now there are 33. This is so obviously the way forward that it will only be a short time before such funerals become the norm. The advantages are very numerous: it is a way of giving the body back to nature; it leads to the planting of more trees, which can only benefit the planet; it avoids the burning of over 400,000 wooden coffins each year and the associated pollution; it provides an income for farmers, for land that would otherwise be set-aside; it avoids filling the countryside with headstones; it is relatively low cost; all the sites allow families to conduct the funeral without using funeral directors, thus allowing for more personal funerals; and all accept cardboard coffins. All those who are members of environmental organisations are likely to prefer this option.

The Natural Death Centre is about to start editing a new edition of the *Natural Death Handbook*. Please let the Centre know your recommendations or warnings about particular funeral directors, funeral suppliers, cemeteries and crematoria.

The Centre's main fundraising book, *Poem for the Day – 366 Poems Old and New Worth Learning by Heart*, which I am proud to have edited, continues to sell extremely well. The publishers, Sinclair-Stevenson, are issuing it as a hardback in November '96, for the Christmas market. In the United States, an American publisher, Steerforth Press, are publishing it in October '96, under the title of *A Poem A Day*, with extra American poems added by my co-editor, the poet Karen

McCosker. Do please consider giving this book as a Christmas present. And do please buy the paperback version of *Poem for the Day* direct from the Natural Death Centre (£11-49 including p&p) as the Centre gains far more this way than through royalties on bookshop sales.

Please also attend the second *Poetry Marathon* in London on Sunday October 13th '96 and recite a poem either for the Natural Death Centre or for the charity of your choice. Your friends and relatives sponsor you to learn any poem by heart and to recite it on stage. Last year's event, with 160 or so adults and 45 children in attendance, was judged a success – "all the people I persuaded to come went away inspired," writes Diana Senior; and Victoria Zinovieff adds: "I felt proud and happy and amazed to find myself up on stage reciting a poem to an audience. It was such a good atmosphere."

For this year, it is hoped that a poem will be engraved on the pavement outside the Amadeus Centre in Little Venice where the event is taking place; and that poems will be hung from trees.

Schools everywhere are being invited to hold their own mini-Poetry Marathons on a date of their choosing. One school last year raised over £2,000 for charity with a week of 'Poetry Happenings'.

- *The Natural Death Centre, 20 Heber Road, London NW2 6AA (tel 0181 208 2853; fax 0181 452 6434; e-mail: <rhino@dial.pipex.com>). This is also the address for the Association of Nature Reserve Burial grounds. Please send £1-56 or six first class stamps for an information pack on 'Inexpensive, Green, Family-Organised Funerals'.*
- *A Poem A Day in the States is available for $15, plus $3 p&p, by credit card from Steerforth Press on 800 639 7140 (PO Box 70, South Royalton, VT 05068).*
- *The Befriending Network, 11 St Bernards Road, Oxford OX2 6EH (tel 01865 316200).*
- *The Poetry Marathon, 20 Heber Road, London NW2 6AA (phone 0181 208 2853 to book a place and to be sent a sponsorship form) at the Amadeus Centre, 50 Shirland Road, Little Venice, London W9, Sunday October 13th '96, 2pm to 6-30pm. The first 50 unemployed people to book in will be paid £10 for the recital of their poem. The first 50 people under 18 will be paid £5.*

PREPARING FOR DYING

What does someone dying need?

Rex Winsbury

Adapted extracts from a document sent to the Befriending Network.

When you get ill and are told you are going to die soon, needs come crowding in on you, jostling for scarce time and (often) scarce energies. So they in turn create their own need, a need for people and places to help you answer your needs. New needs then spring up as you begin to grasp the imperatives of dying.

> **'I was declared to be dying and did not. I experienced the needs and the challenges, and lived to reflect on them'**

My position is odd – not unique, but privileged. I was declared to be dying, and did not. I experienced the needs and the challenges, and lived to reflect on them afterwards. A temporary reprieve, of unknowable duration. Those needs and challenges have not gone away, but I can now look at them with some benefit of hindsight. So I could sum up the needs of one person diagnosed as close to death, me, as being:

- The need to 'settle up' with the people that I felt close to, so as to die in peace, with them and with myself.
- The need to have someone to 'stand in' for me, to do what I could not do when I became helpless or consigned to the grave.
- The need for places and organisations that I could turn to for practical information.
- The need for someone to guide me, or go with me, round this new and unfamiliar domain of 'the terminal state' – not necessarily the same someone for every sector of it.

Finances

I was lucky in having, already, an expert professional financial adviser who, as it turned out, could talk about death as a human being as well as help me plan for it as a financial consultant. I had also had the benefit, before my diagnosis, of talks with a psychotherapist, who had taught me something about the inner and outer processes of reconciliation.

Settling up emotional accounts

Settling up emotional accounts means going to those people who have been hurt by you, betrayed by you, misled by you, and not just asking forgiveness (because that is to perpetuate the desire to control the outcome by laying down what the outcome is going to be) but asking them to tell you how the hurt may be healed.

> **'Settling up emotional accounts means going to those people who have been hurt by you, betrayed by you, misled by you'**

Once you have opened that door to them, given them that permission, you cannot control what will then happen. People will react in surprising, sometimes offensive,

---

Creative Endings, £5-95 by credit card from The Natural Death Centre, tel London 0181 208 2853

sometimes heart-stirring ways – but almost always in ways of their own choosing, which is the key to the success of this exercise.

The role of advocate

If you are ill, maybe in pain, perhaps drugged, perhaps even on life-support, someone needs to represent you to the doctors and nurses, the medical profession, to say what you would have said if you had been able, about your treatment, about where you want to live your last days and die, and what treatment you would (if you could) accept or refuse. This is about life-support; about pain; about dying with dignity; about relating your death to those who care about you.

> **'If you are ill, someone needs to represent you to the doctors'**

I have a partner who would have played, and will play, that role with determination.

Drawing up an ethical will

An ethical (as well as a financial) will is a key document to have at life's frontier post. In an ethical will, you can say how and where you want to die, and in what medical circumstances. An ethical will help the person who 'stands in' for you to argue the case with the doctors, and maybe the lawyers. It can say what sort of funeral you want. It can (if not done separately) give your last messages to those who matter to you. But there are no lawyers to draw up ethical wills on pre-prepared forms. There are, however, others who can advise on how to draw up an ethical will. So here there are three stages. The first is to recognise the need for such a will. The second is to find advice on how to write one. The third is the most difficult – to actually write it. I dithered for months, afraid of the decisions implied in the clauses of an ethical will. But again, once done, it was a relief.

I obtained advice from the Natural Death Centre, and specimen ethical wills from the Terence Higgins Trust and from the Rigpa Buddhist Centre, all in London. I drew, eclectically, from each.

The funeral

Someone, if I have not done it already, needs to make my funeral arrangements, in accordance with the advice in my Will, but subject always to the law of the land about dead bodies. Not everyone can cope with these last practicalities, which is why undertakers make a good living by applying a fixed ritual, and fixed price, to death. Some people care more than others about these post-mortem rituals, and how to redesign them in your own image. I myself care little, except to avoid more than basic expenses. Keep me from an expensive coffin.

I obtained valuable advice and ideas about these matters from the Natural Death Centre, in London.

One-stop-shop

I needed a place where I could go, there and then, if I fell ill again, if I began to die, confident that I would be known, understood, cared for, well advised medically, and listened to: somewhere I trusted, and where I would be treated as a full human being. There is a peace in knowing that there is such a place to go, if and when ... and that there is someone who will take you there.

Such a place proved to be, alas, not a conventional hospital, but a Marie Curie Centre, where care is more than drugs and surgery, where pain can be controlled, where I am more than a numbered patient, and which is, but is far more than, a hospice for dying in.

Need to know

You need somewhere to turn to for basic information. Ignorance is the worst enemy. Some prefer ignorance, say it is bliss. It is not. Ignorance is the ultimate fright, the primal fear. Better to know what you are up against, know all there is to know about your illness, its treatments, the odds, the therapies, what others have done and said and suffered. But where is that place? Not everyone knows, or bothers to tell you. Just like a second opinion, knowledge can also be scary.

'You need somewhere to turn to for information on the disease'

I spent a terrified afternoon in a bookshop, looking up the medical statistics about survival rates for people with my specific form of cancer. You cannot, must not wish that sort of knowledge on people who cannot cope with it. On the other hand, for those who grasp the power of knowledge, knowing the statistics can liberate you from the tyranny of being just a statistic.

For example, for those with cancer, CancerLink and Bacup, both in London, provide information and counselling. It is not always as specific as I would like. Faced with illness, soothing generalisations are all too easy to fall into. But both organisations are invaluable.

A safe place to talk

Family and friends are often reluctant to face up to illness and death: even if they are not, their experience is not your experience, cannot be. So you may need, as I did, somewhere to go where you can talk, where it is safe to expose your inmost fears and terrors, your hopes and vulnerability. A group of people with similar vulnerabilities can provide that safe place, and be a powerful haven in which to bring out repressed feelings. It can support and share. But where is that group, and is it really safe? There are lists of Support Groups, but you may need help to get to one, even if there is one near enough.

Finding no cancer support group in my area, I started one. It has become a haven, both for me and for some dozens of others. I am sad that more people do not come to it.

Physical wellbeing

When your body is in danger, you need to do what you can to restore it, to prolong its utility, to seek to repair that wholeness that has been compromised by illness. Being diagnosed as terminally ill, does not always or necessarily mean that your physical activity has ceased, or cannot be prolonged. It is not too late. But where can you go to learn to repair what is damaged? Once again, this quest presupposes the will to do it, the same willingness that is inherent in many other felt needs, the willingness to plan for the future while knowing that you may not be there to see it.

But now, at the point of terminal diagnosis, more than ever, your need is to nurture your physical wellbeing by any means, to make the most of what you have left. But how? Exercise, diet? What exercise, what diet? Where is the place to discover this, and to do it? Probably, a conventional gymnasium is useless at this stage: hospitals are little use. Where can an ill person go to improve his or her physique? There are places, and which of them is a matter of knowing, and of choice, and the will.

> 'I found great healing power in walking on Hampstead Heath and in Chinese Qi Gong classes'

I myself found great healing power, as well as physical exercise, in walking or jogging on Hampstead Heath, London, and in Chinese Qi Gong classes – both of these activities combine movement and meditation.

Guides and other special people

In additional to the financial and emotional advisers described earlier, I needed:

(1) Someone or somewhere to talk about death.
(2) Someone to tell me I am still beautiful.
(3) Someone who would help to restore my hope, within the context of realism about my situation.
(4) Someone to forewarn me and teach me about the stress of my illness upon others.
(5) Someone to recognise and encourage the emergence of that new, alternative person that might never have been born without that illness and diagnosis:

Creative Endings, £5-95 by credit card from The Natural Death Centre, tel London 0181 208 2853

someone who will teach me to understand the power of the ill person, both over him/herself and over others – a power to be used wisely and humanely, for it can be, if misused, a tyranny, both over oneself and over others.

The Rigpa Buddhist Centre and the Natural Death Centre in London provided (1).

My partner (miraculously, considering my operation scars) did (2).

I found the Bristol Cancer Help Centre very helpful in relation to (3).

(4) was a problem – in the months after diagnosis I was too angry, too self-preoccupied to want to know about the stress on others: when they told me about it, I did not listen. It was a year before I was ready to even try to deal with it. But perhaps someone could have opened my ears earlier.

As to (5) – it is something I have come to learn from many conversations, encounters, my own experience, and many books, not least some of those written by Oliver Sacks.

Epitaph

Having feared death all my life, now that I am confronted with it, I no longer fear it, only that the period leading up to death (a period whose duration, trickily, I do not know) will have been a waste. Had I during my life feared death as little as I do now, I would have dared more and better things. Only slowly is the power conferred by loss of that fear, growing upon me. Partly, this is because I am afraid of that loss of fear. Where will it take me? My final need is to find out that last truth. That is one need that, I suspect, no one else can help with.

Rex Winsbury, 52 Brookfield Mansions, London N6 6AT (tel 0181 347 6713).

Joy within the crevices of cancer and fear

Fine Black Lines *by Lois Tschetter Hjelmstad (published by Mulberry Hill Press, 1993, ISBN 0 9637139 5 7, 166 pages). Reviewed by Nicholas Albery.*

Fine Black Lines is a thoughtful and inspiring book, self-published by Lois Tschetter Hjelmstad and a worthy winner of the Colorado Independent Publishers Award. The poetry in the book is first class. The journal reflections on facing cancer, fear and loneliness are moving and profound. The book, which tells the story of Lois Hjelmstad's diagnosis of breast cancer, of her Chronic Fatigue Syndrome, double mastectomy and other ordeals, would make a very appropriate present for any family touched by cancer, despite its lack of a completely 'happy ending'. The author's belief that it is possible to find some joy in almost every human experience shines through in every page.

I can only be surprised that this book has not been snapped up by a British publisher. In the meantime, British readers can obtain the book quite simply by sending their credit card details to the address below. Here, to entice you to do so, are some extracts that enlightened or moved me.

Diagnosis

When I was first diagnosed with breast cancer, all I could think of was that I had known at least twelve women who had died of breast cancer, and I could think of only two who had survived. Since then, I have met many survivors and now know that when breast cancer is detected and treated early, the chances of five-year survival are 80% or better.

A commitment to keeping sex alive

Many years ago, while waiting in a doctor's office, I saw an article in Reader's Digest about making a commitment to keeping sex alive in marriage. It grabbed my interest, so I brought it home, and Les and I discussed it at length. We had always had a lively and passionate physical relationship, so it almost seemed ridiculous to make such a promise, but we did.

> **'Commitment to keeping sex alive has served us well over the years'**

The promise has served us well over the years. We made our dates and faithfully kept them, working around Les's night shift for 26 years: when there were teenagers in the house, when time pressures overwhelmed us, when back surgery and a broken pelvis required some ingenuity.

The promise serves us well now – especially now. There are days when it seems almost hopeless to even try to keep sex alive in our marriage. The obstacles seem almost impossible to overcome – the lack of libido, the drenching hot flashes, the lingering surgical pain, and the feeling of ugliness that will not go away, no matter how much Les reassures me that I am beautiful.

But by honouring our commitment, we still share tenderness, love, joy, and yes, ecstasy, especially ecstasy.

The gift

>   It is a gift—
>   this reminder of mortality
>   this thing that slows me down
>   this reflective summer
>
>   I know things about myself
>   I could not otherwise have known—
>   pain can be endured

Creative Endings, £5-95 by credit card from *The Natural Death Centre*, tel London 0181 208 2853

      uncertainty can be tolerated
      loss can be processed

I know there is a well-spring of
    strength
    courage
    joy   within me

I know that time is not forever
There is
    an urgency
    a poignancy
    a preciousness   to life

I know that I do not fear
    suffering or death
    as much   any more

It is a menace
It is a sorrow
It is a loss of innocence
                it is a gift

No Lifeguard on Duty

    it is difficult
    when one is drowning
    to wave to the people
    on shore

    one wants to be
    friendly, of course,

    But perhaps it is
    more important
    to keep
    swimming

Necessity

    some things cannot be fixed
      sometimes we simply
        have to reinvent
          our lives

Creative Endings, £5-95 by credit card from *The Natural Death Centre, tel London 0181 208 2853*

What can I say? [Extract]

... Shall I say
    Keep up your courage
    (you who have been so courageous)?
    Keep up your strength
    (you who have been so strong)?

But we know that courage sometimes falters
And strength is not always ours to grasp

What can I say to you, my friend?
Perhaps I shall say nothing—
    I'll press you to my wounded breast
    hold you ever in my thoughts
    and hope you know how much I love you...

Afterlife

Someday there will be
A tunnel of Light

I will find it and
Walk toward it

At the very least
I may find cessation

I hope
I may find joy

I am willing
to find   what is

The limitations of positive thinking

People often charge cancer (and other) patients to "think positively". Meaning well, some even give us books that become oppressive with hints that we are responsible for becoming ill and for getting well again.

"Push away that negative thought!"

"You must think positively."

    I have had several friends who heard and read similar things and who worked very hard to maintain an optimistic attitude in the face of some very discouraging facts. Eventually they all died – each having to deal with more than a destroyed body. I admired their courage, but felt very sad that they bore this additional burden.

Creative Endings, £5-95 by credit card from *The Natural Death Centre, tel London 0181 208 2853*

Sometimes when I tried to break through the barrier, to get them to talk about what they were really thinking and feeling, they seemed afraid to even mention the possibility of not getting well, as though that would be a jinx.

Did they think they were causing their illness? Did they blame themselves for not thinking positively enough?

I believe there is a mind-body connection. Our attitudes certainly affect the quality of our lives. I very much believe in living in a positive way. My game plan has been to carry on my life, continue as much of my teaching and writing as possible, enjoy every moment I can.

'Facing limitations, accepting them and working round them has helped me'

But I also believe in reality. And regardless of what the best approach might be for others, I have found that facing limitations, accepting them, and working around them has helped me to cope.

It works out better some days than others.

Judgement call

> I am willing to spend a day teaching children
> But I am not willing to track investments.
> It was one thing when I had
> All the time in the world.
> It is another thing now.
>
> I am willing to cook a tasty meal
> But I am not willing to be served in a restaurant.
> It was one thing when I had
> All the patience in the world.
> It is another thing now.
>
> I am willing to listen to another's pain
> But I am not willing to chit-chat over lunch.
> It was one thing when
> Any subject interested me.
> It is another thing now.
>
> I am willing to walk two miles in the woods
> But I am not willing to hunt for bargain.
> It was one thing when I had
> All the strength in the world.
> It is another thing now.
> I am grateful to discover the difference

Creative Endings, £5-95 by credit card from The Natural Death Centre, tel London 0181 208 2853

Between things that matter to me –
And things that do not.

The men in our lives

Breast cancer is hard on the men in our lives. They must deal not only with the fear of losing us, but also with the tedium and trauma of treatments and our shifting moods as we confront our mortality. We often pull away from them because we cannot bear the possibility of rejection.

> 'I'm thinking about death – and you're thinking about sex?'

Sometimes conflicts arise from different ways of coping. One husband shared with Les his despair that when he expressed a desire to make love, his wife retorted, "I'm thinking about death – and you're thinking about sex?" She didn't understand his need for intimacy, and he didn't understand her fear of mortality.

Joy in imperfection

I realized I have changed. Now I tell my music students (and myself) that the walls will not cave in if we mis-play a few notes – the important thing is to create beauty and joy, to give it our best and to have fun while we are doing it.

> 'The walls will not cave in if we mis-play a few notes – the important thing is to create beauty and joy'

Perhaps it is only when we truly understand that our lives will not be perfect that we have the freedom to venture into the rose garden, without worrying about scratches from the thorns.

For me, a happy ending is the knowledge that, even though the flame may flicker, my inner candle of joy burns brightly.

I have found an immense awareness, an incredible joy in treasuring each moment – and a profound gratitude that greets each day as if it were the First Morning.

'Fine Black Lines' is available from bookshops at $14-95. To order direct from the UK, phone (or send your credit card number – Mastercard or Visa – and expiry date) to: Mulberry Hill Press, Box 425 B, Englewood, CO 80151, USA (tel 001 800 294 4714).

18 Creative Endings

Homesharers

Adapted and updated from an item in Information Exchange newsletter (July '95).

Homesharing is a scheme run by the Community Care Trust, whose aim is to provide good and inexpensive care to elderly, disabled people. With homesharing, the disadvantaged householder provides free accommodation in their home to a Homesharer, who in return, provides help in the home, for example help with cooking, cleaning, shopping and other tasks, and the assurance that someone will be there at night.

Homesharers continue their usual occupation; most are professional people, some from overseas, who wish to work or study in London. There is a thorough selection and matching process. Over thirty 'pairings' are in place, mainly in Central London, Kingston and Richmond.

'Free accommodation in return for help'

But of particular interest, was the organisation's intention, currently dormant, of making a special effort to help those with life-threatening illnesses.

A well-supported carer makes a major difference to a person's ability to contemplate dying at home; a Homesharer could offer continuity and personalised care, as well as friendship.

The Trust had planned to offer an educational package designed to familiarise Homesharers with issues specific to terminal care, as well as more general care issues.

If the Householder were being cared for by a family member, the ability to share the night calls and support one another would be invaluable. By offering the space in their home, the Householder would feel involved in their own care.

Further information from: Mrs G McKinnel, Homeshare, St Mary Abbots Church House, Vicarage Gate, London W8 4HN (tel 0171 376 0111).

Keep family informed every 15 minutes

Two adapted extracts from a review by Kelly Osmont in Death Studies journal (subs £45 from Taylor & Francis Ltd, 1 Gunpowder Sqaure, London EC4A 3DE) of Death Notification: a practical guide to the process *by R. Moroni Leash (published by Upper Access, Hinesburg, Vermont, 1994, ISBN 0 942679 08 3, $19.95).*

When a patient in hospital is alive, and the medical staff is working on a revival, Leash, a medical social worker, suggests that family members should be kept informed every 15 minutes "to alleviate anxiety and convey to the family that everything possible is being done for their loved one".

Creative Endings, £5-95 by credit card from The Natural Death Centre, tel London 0181 208 2853

Whisper goodbye

And when the battle is lost?
  Leash writes:
    With all the hurrying that goes on, somehow the patient becomes a thing. So when we know they're not going to be saved, I like to lean down and whisper goodbye. It's the one time I let my guard down. They're checking out, and why not make them feel better about it.

Hospital cleaners to care for terminally ill

Adapted extracts from an article by Lois Rogers, entitled 'Hospital cleaners to take over care for terminally ill', in The Sunday Times. Incidentally, no one should underestimate the importance of the hospital cleaner: there was a research study which found that, when children in hospital were asked to rate the staff in order of importance to them, the surgeons came bottom and the cleaners came top.

Hospital cleaners at the Royal Hallamshire Hospital in Sheffield are taking over caring for terminally ill patients as part of a 'multi-skilling' exercise. They will combine mopping toilets with bathing patients and other duties currently performed by nursing support staff.

The cleaners, who are to be re-designated 'generic workers', are to undergo a training course to equip them for the new healthcare responsibilities; it will last a month. They will then be allowed to perform blood and temperature checks, and to bathe and feed patients. They will be expected to continue cleaning ward areas, corridors and toilets and distributing drinks and meals.

Initially five nursing support workers at the hospital will be replaced by domestic staff on a ward caring for 33 terminally ill adult patients.

A hundred pages of forms for your last wishes

Last wishes – a workbook for recording your funeral, memorial and other final instructions *by Lucinda Page Knoz and Michael D. Knox (published by Applied Science Corporation, PO Box 16118, Tampa, FL 33687-6118, USA; for credit card orders phone 001 800 356 9315; fax 001 813 988; $17-95 incl. p&p, $5 extra for orders from outside North America).*

Last Wishes consists of a rather intimidating hundred pages of forms that a person can fill in before death, to make life easier for the survivors. The authors were motivated to complete the book by the death of a close relative and the difficulties of tracking down all the relevant documents and also having to plan the funeral without any knowledge of their relative's preferences.

There are spaces for details of one's partners, children, siblings, past jobs, honours and accomplishments; for the addresses of those to be notified, whether friends, colleagues, associations or churches; for information to be included in an obituary; for the distribution of small personal items; for special messages to family and friends; and for funeral arrangements, including preferred poetry, music, flowers, donations, pallbearers, viewing preferences, clothes for the body, disposal of remains, inscription and design for a headstone.

On the legal and financial side, there are details to fill in about Power of Attorney, the Will and Living Will, safe deposit box and key, insurance policies, bank accounts, certificates of deposit, investment accounts, stocks, bonds and mutual funds, other sources of income, major business and property holdings, and debts owed and owing.

Then there are bibliographies, addresses of useful organisations and some light-hearted quotes.

My criticism of this otherwise comprehensive book is that it tends towards the norm rather than encouraging alternatives. There is nothing about what the person might like to have in their surroundings whilst dying; nothing in the wording of the forms offering the option of funeral without funeral director; or private land burial; or trees instead of headstones; or home-made coffins; or one-flower-per-person at the funeral; or obituaries on the Internet. The examples of obituaries given are as boring as boring can be.

I think that people might get as much stimulation on many of these matters from the 4 page set of forms from the Natural Death Centre (Living Will, values statement, death plan and advance funeral wishes forms) than from this monster book; and for the rest, one really only needs the list of the book's contents, as above, to be able to leave one's own personalised instructions. The more d-i-y the better.

The set of forms mentioned cost four first class UK stamps, or equivalent money, from The Natural Death Centre, 20 Heber Road, London NW2 6AA (tel 0181 208 2853; fax 0181 452 6434; e-mail <rhino@dial.pipex.com>).

'Being with dying' – model projects
Joan Halifax

Adapted extracts from an article in The Quest (Autumn '95; Quest is the magazine of the Theosophical Society of America), monitored for the Natural Death Centre by Kevin Core. Joan Halifax has written a new book called Being with Dying *and is the founder of Upaya, a Buddhist Centre in Santa Fe, New Mexico, where she works with dying people.*

Each week I sit with a group of people, some of whom are dying, some of whom are care givers. I have worked with dying people for 25 years. I sit and listen.

In this work, I am defined in various ways: as a Buddhist priest doing pastoral work, as a medical anthropologist, as a care giver, as a friend. I prefer the last because I do not want to be distanced by roles and titles. I am simply a person in the community who brings a certain quality of mindfulness and compassion to those who are suffering.

From one point of view, there is nothing special about what I do. I do what any care giver does, what any friend or relative might do, for one who is suffering or dying. These activities range from sitting in ease and silence for long periods with a dying person, to giving a sponge bath or foot rub to alleviate discomfort, to entering the questions around dying that many people are fearful of asking or exploring. People want a peaceful death, a gentle death. We all want to die well.

We in the West need to articulate a psychological and philosophical foundation, a point of view, and a practice for working with the dying process.

'There are things we can do that help the true nature of dying come forth'

Dying is a completely natural event. But there are things we can do, ways we can be that help the true nature of dying come forth. These 'ways of being' are expressed in terms such as compassion, tolerance, ease, kindness, humour, warmth, wisdom, authenticity, mindfulness, stability, openness, concentration. These are qualities of a psychologically and spiritually mature person. How are these qualities fostered in our culture? What can we do to open these sensibilities within our communities, so family members and friends can have the internal means to work with suffering in a compassionate and skilful manner?

Dying well is not only for ourselves, but also those who survive us.

Death is not an individual act. The dying person is a performer in a drama that will be observed by others and participated in by others. Like the last will and testament we leave upon our deaths to materially benefit those who survive us, we also leave a legacy of how we have experienced our own death.

We need to develop and support programmes for care givers, dying people and professionals that are based in a contemplative perspective and that offer spiritual care.

Training in contemplative approaches and practices is important at the professional level, where dying and death are encountered on a daily basis, and where the pressure of work and 'patient load' is great. It should be a core element of the medical curriculum.

We need to identify already existing groups and institutions that are doing this type of contemplative work and infuse them with support to deepen and expand their efforts. This would include Christian and Jewish groups and congregations, elder community volunteers, hospice groups, and so on. Grassroots work can be very effective because this is not only where dying is happening, this is where low cost, effective support can be given.

'Training in contemplative work with the dying needs to be developed'

Training in contemplative work with the dying needs to be developed. An inter-cultural and inter-religious group should be formed to accept the challenge to create culturally relevant, flexible, and effective training and care giving programmes in spiritual care for the dying that are appropriate for different cultural contexts.

• Just as there is sex education in the school system, there should be education in the awareness of death and dying, which should cover not only the physiology of dying, but also its cultural, spiritual, and psychological dimensions. There should be a curriculum to train young people and adults in the awareness of death.

• Programmes in community building around the issue of death and dying should be created. Such programmes can deepen relationships in the community, and can deepen inquiry, making genuine and effective support more available. It can alleviate care giving families, who are under great stress and pressure, take some of the work load off the professional community, and put dying where it most often should be – in the home and community with loved ones.

'Projects using a contemplative and spiritual basis should be created, supported, and evaluated as to their effectiveness'

• Model projects using a contemplative and spiritual basis should be created, supported, and evaluated as to their effectiveness in helping dying persons and their families, care givers and physicians.

• There should be a computer network for dying people and care givers where information and support can be given.

• Small group meetings should be supported for the exchange of ideas among care giving and physician groups. Dying people should be included in such meetings.

• It is important to support the development of pharmaceuticals to manage pain that do not diminish mental acuity. It is also important to explore contemplative techniques for dealing with severe pain.

• There should be a wide range of audio, video, and CD programs for care givers and dying people on aspects of dying process, including contemplative work with the dying.

Editorial note: In the UK, the Befriending Network attempts to build community networks to support those who are dying – and is in need of volunteer visitors. The Befriending Network, 11 St Bernards Road, Oxford OX2 6EH (tel 01865 316200).

Creative Endings, £5-95 by credit card from The Natural Death Centre, tel London 0181 208 2853

Designer dying, Leary-style

Timothy Leary, the 60s champion of LSD, died on May 31st '96. The following adapted extracts are from a conversation between Tim Leary and Laura Mansnerus, entitled 'At death's door, the message is tune in, turn on, drop in', in the New York Times (Nov 26th '95) monitored for the Institute by Roger Knights.

Dying, for Timothy Leary, is the experience of a lifetime. "It's called designer dying," he explained. "It's a hip, chic, vogue thing to do. It's the most elegant thing you can do."

He learned in January '96 that he had an inoperable prostrate cancer, whereupon he called his old Harvard colleague Ram Dass, among others, to share "the wonderful news" and began the "directed dying" that he had been writing about for 20 years.

"I'm looking forward to the most fascinating experience in life, which is dying," he said. "You've got to approach your dying the way you live your life – with curiosity, with hope, with fascination, with courage and with the help of your friends."

'Let us have no more pious, wimpy talk about death. The time has come to talk cheerfully and joke sassily'

In his latest book, *Chaos and Cyber Culture* (Ronin Publishing, 1994), Leary wrote: "Let us have no more pious, wimpy talk about death. The time has come to talk cheerfully and joke sassily about personal responsibility for managing the dying process." And he wrote about "creative alternatives to going belly-up clutching the company logo of the Christian Cross."

Leary is setting up his own event at home, in his bed, with particular attention to that sliver of time between life and death, or near-death and death.

"When you heart stops beating, there's a period of 3 to 15 minutes while your brain is still alive," he said. "It's that period that's never really been explored ... I can't wait for the moment when I'll have the experience of being in my brain without my body being around," he said. "I'm working on ways of sending signals, my eyebrows moving, that sort of thing."

'Do not be alone. Dying is a team sport. People will learn from my experience of dying'

When dying, he advises, "do not be alone. Dying is a team sport. It may be a farce, but people will learn from my experience of dying."

He continues to deride authorities of all kings. "I would say to everybody, do not let the priests and popes and medics tell you what to do."

The drugs that eased Leary's dying days

Joan Halifax (see previous article) writes of the needs for pharmaceuticals for those who are dying that do not reduce mental acuity. The following is a list of Timothy Leary's daily intake of drugs during the week of April 14th to April 21st '96 – seven weeks before he died. This list appeared in the LA Weekly (May 17th '96) monitored for the Natural Death Centre by Greg Wright.

During the week, he smoked 50 cigarettes, and consumed two Dilaulid, two lines of coke, 45 cc of ketamine, an unspecified amount of DMT, a phentynol patch, 12 balloons of nitrous oxide, and two Leary Biscuits – made by adding a lump of butter or cheese to a Ritz cracker, topping it with a fresh marijuana bud, and heating it until the cheese or butter melts and the THC comes alive.

Dr Timothy Leary's Web page about his ideas and works is still maintained by his friends at the location <http://www.leary.com:8081/news/news.html>. He was preparing a final book, The Ultimate Trip – A manual for Designer Dying, due to be published by Harper Collins, in the Spring of '97.

Do people die as they've lived?

La mort intime by Marie de Hennezel, with a preface by François Mitterrand (published in Paris by Robert Laffont, 1995, ISBN 2 221 07830 6, 109 French francs).

Marie de Hennezel, the author of La mort intime (which has yet to be translated into English), is the psychologist who helped the late French President, François Mitterrand, face his approaching death with such courage; and to use it as an opportunity to unravel knots from his past – for instance, to be more open about his compromising wartime encounters with members of the Vichy regime and to reveal his secret illegitimate daughter. Mitterrand writes in the preface that "this book's finest teaching is that sometimes dying can help a being to find fulfilment, dying can be an accomplishment". In the event, Mitterrand took his dying under his control at the very end, by deciding against accepting further medicine or food.

The following is a free translation of an adapted extract from Marie de Hennezel's book.

"Do people die as they've lived?" an old friend of mine asked. I remembered Dürckheim, who'd spent his life learning and teaching a form of Buddhism and yet who died after a year of agony, struggle and resistance – just the opposite of that radiant serenity which used to draw spiritual seekers to him.

So do people die as they've lived? I could still be tempted to believe it and yet for my part, the most beautiful death I have witnessed was that of a young addict woman of 25, suffering from advanced breast cancer, who had lived, she said, "the life of a galley-slave". On her bald head was a tattoo with the inscription "Walk or die". She had had a childhood without love, and a hard, almost absurd life.

Abandoned at birth by her prostitute mother, brought up by her grandmother, she had developed like a wildflower, thirsting for love and the absolute, and finding whatever she could to quench her thirst. She had, she said, tried everything. She was without illusions. Her cancer in some ways had brought hope: hope that at last her wretched existence would end – her drugs of addiction hadn't yet had time to kill her.

If death were indeed to come as a reflection of her life, this woman's death could be a difficult and rebellious death, or at least an anguished one. But in fact it worked out differently.

'She had asked her mother to bring a bottle of champagne, which the two of them drank, remembering the good times, despite everything'

One morning I was at her bedside. She said she was about to die. The day before, she had asked her mother to bring a bottle of champagne, which the two of them had drunk, remembering the good times they'd had together, despite everything. This had been her way of saying goodbye to this woman who had abandoned her, but who remained her mother.

I was there at her side at Dr Clement's request, given that she had announced that she was going to die. The young woman was lying on her back, her head slightly lifted on the pillow. Her lungs were hardly functioning and she had oxygen tubes in her nostrils. Her breathing was difficult and noisy. On her naked front, there was a wet face cloth for relieving her fever. As I took her hand, I noticed that she was indeed burning with heat.

She wanted to speak with me, but her voice was feeble. I brought my ear close to her lips. I distinctly heard her say, "I am going to die".

'She went into a birthing position. Her breathing became short and more and more noisy'

With one decided movement, she pulled out the oxygen tubes and threw them beyond the face cloth. Whilst I looked on stonily, she went into a birthing position, with her legs apart. Her breathing became short and more and more noisy. But she seemed calm and did not seem to be suffering.

For several minutes, I asked myself if I should put the oxygen back, but her action had been so decisive and she seemed so calm, that I decided to do nothing, except to stay with her, so that she would not be alone. She repeated "I am going to die". I started to caress her, whilst she panted. And it was as if she were pushing with her legs, as if giving birth.

Michel de M'uzan's words came into my mind, about the interior work accomplished by someone who is dying: "it is an attempt to bring oneself completely into the world before disappearing." Now, for the first time, these

---
Creative Endings, £5-95 by credit card from The Natural Death Centre, tel London 0181 208 2853

words had a real meaning for me. This young woman, who had had such a lot of trouble living, was she not bringing herself into the world, giving birth to herself? I felt tenderness and awe.

She could have been my daughter and I held her and spoke comforting, motherly words to her, words coming from the soul of all mothers, from infinity. Several times she swallowed a little air. The image of a poor fish floundering on the sand was in my mind. I would have like to have put her back in the water. I would have liked to give her life. Tears came to my eyes. A third time she stopped breathing and all at once the tension left her body. I realised she had died.

We too could wish to die with such awareness and such dignity.

Stocking up on beauty

Adapted extracts from an interview by Alex Duval Smith with Marie de Hennezel, entitled 'The art of dying', in the Guardian (Sept 28th '95).

I have treated two priests. They were among my most anxious patients. Faith does not help you to die. Confidence in life does.

Accompanying the dying has taught me to appreciate life in the moment it is lived. What wears us out is bearing the burden of thought for the past or the future. I have also learnt to relax. I enjoy country walks, singing and beauty. The dying want to sap a great deal from the living. It is my duty to stock up on these things – beauty, life, pleasure – so that I can give it to those I am accompanying.

The good death

The good death – conversations with East Londoners *by Michael Young and Lesley Cullen (published by Routledge, 1996, ISBN 0 415 13797 7). Reviewed by Nicholas Albery.*

In the olden days, people embarking on a challenging enterprise might consult the Oracle at Delphi. Michael Young's way of writing a book is similar – he interviews a few East Londoners (in this latest book on death and dying, he interviewed 14 in all) and uses their remarks and experience as the foundation for an edifying mix of philosophising and recommendations.

In this book, many of the resulting observations are commonplaces about death and dying and would read almost as clichés, but are saved by his poet's eye and his knack as a social inventor for proposing just the new institution or measure that might help. Indeed, he is unable to stop himself – the preface gives an account of his wife Sasha, dying from cancer, and how he was able to distract himself with social activism "as I am always liable to do". As President of the College of Health, he tries to help save Barts, the hospital where Sasha was being treated, from closure. He had also taken "the almost laughable course of setting up a National Funerals College to improve the conduct of funerals".

Sasha's funeral

He describes Sasha's beautiful funeral in the great medieval church of St Bartholomew-the-Great:

> **'The funeral director invited each person to place a single flower on her body'**

Sasha lay in an open coffin ... The funeral director, Mr Cribb, invited each person to place a single flower on her body. There was music and poetry reading and chanting by brown-robed monks and talks by our two children, Toby as well as Sophie. The last poem of hers to be read was 'The Company of the Birds'

> Ah the company of the birds
> I loved and cherished on Earth
> Now, freed of flesh we fly
> Together, a flock of beating wings,
> I am as light, as feathery,
> As gone from gravity we soar
> In endless circles.

Afterwards in the cemetery there was a long silence amongst her friends as Sasha's body was lowered into the grave. The human silence was filled with the singing of what seemed like a chorus of innumerable birds.

The force of social gravity

Michael Young (and his co-author Lesley Cullen) describe how the imminence of death can induce "a kind of solidarity amongst neighbours ... Death is not only an extraordinary event for the dying but brings out extraordinary behaviour in other people". They adduce this altruism to a latent sense of unity within society:

> **'A weaker but universal force of gravity, of social gravity, which is always acting to hold people together'**

Underlying all the stronger forces which keep societies in being – the common traditions, the common languages, the common interests, the hierarchies of power – is a weaker but universal force of gravity, of social gravity, which is always acting to hold people together ... It can draw people not only to others who are still alive but to others who have died before.

In view of the book's stress on care for dying at home, I wish there had been space in its four appendices to mention the Befriending Network, founded by the

Natural Death Centre, which is trying to encourage priests and doctors and other opinion leaders in any locality to organise rotas of neighbours to care for the dying in their homes and to relieve the carers by running errands.

The authors do at least argue for an expansion of Home Care nursing help "so that present regional and local inequalities can be reduced, and more people in more places (and not just sufferers from cancer) get the benefit of the kind of home service which was available to our [East London] patients".

The individualist's right to be in control

Michael Young, working with the College of Health, once prepared a scheme for a hospital where patients on their discharge had an interview. They were told why they had been admitted, what had been found and what had been done to them, and what they and their family could do to help them at home. Patients were also sent home with a tape of the conversation, which many found particularly valuable.

> 'Patients were also sent home with a tape of the conversation, which many found particularly valuable'

Michael Young, as co-founder of the Consumers' Association, is thus well aware of the need to empower the individual consumer. He quotes a research project where 95% of patients wanted to be told if they had cancer. The rights of the individual are clear in this instance.

But it leaves Michael Young in a quandary on the issue of euthanasia – on the one hand, there is "the individual's right to die, the individual's right to know and to decide". On the other hand, families would have to agree to euthanasia. They might feel responsible and guilty, "they would be bound to ask themselves whether the death was the result of their lack of love". It could also "undermine the trust that people feel, and need to feel, in their doctors". (He fails to deal with the more convincing 'slippery slope' argument that acceptance of killing, and killing itself, feeds on killing, just as the Nazis started with killing a few mental patients and went on to gassing millions of Jews, or just as the Roman emperors started with gladiators and ended up, for their entertainment, with blind people in the arena hacking each other to the death with swords.) So although "the main drift of this book is against euthanasia", he and his co-author, after much wavering, come down finally in favour: "It is high time for the most stringent safeguards to be worked out and incorporated in the law".

Actors without parts to play

The book argues for new traditions and for new churches to fill the void that surrounds dying today.

At most contemporary deaths, the mourners and others are actors without any lines, participants in a drama without parts to play. They can be hollow people.

Dying, indeed, sometimes seems easier for the dying person than for the survivors. A quick death, say the authors, "is no boon for the bereaved", leaving no time mentally and emotionally to prepare for the disaster. And yet "a good death (or at least a prolonged death) for the patient may work in exactly the opposite way for the bereaved". The carer becomes so tired, she or he cannot lift themselves up. The authors quote a study which implicates bereavement in the causation of several types of cancer.

How, then, can a 'good death' help?

The dying could help the bereaved by returning the love so that it remained a comfort after the death, and as real (or almost as real) as it had been in life. The person who dies in peace, with acceptance rather than bitterness, bestows a gift upon the survivors which lasts for them, and can quieten their own fears.

'Comeditation' – exhaling together with sounds

Adapted extracts from a book by Richard W. Boerstler and Hulen S. Kornfield, entitled Life to Death, Harmonizing the Transition *(published by Healing Arts Press, One Park Street, Rochester, Vermont, USA, tel 001 800 246 8648; distributed to the book trade in the UK by Deep Books, London; 1995, ISBN 0 89281 329 6, 240 pages, $10-95 plus $3 p&p).*

Comeditation is a technique which can relieve the pain and anxiety felt by any individual, even one who is seriously ill. Most especially, it can ease the transition experienced by one who is dying. Though an ancient practice originally developed in Tibet, the technique is suitable for use in our time and society.

'Following progressive relaxation, the recipient and the assistant make the sound "ahhh" together'

The word comeditation signifies meditation with another. In actual practice, the primary person is the one who receives the method. The primary meditator – the recipient – assumes a position as nearly straight and flat on the back as is comfortable. The second person – the assistant – serves as a guide to prompt a progressive muscle relaxation process and to make sound cues when the recipient exhales. Following progressive relaxation, the recipient and the assistant make the sound 'ahhh' together.

The exhalation of old air clears the lungs of both participants, while the echoing effect of the doubled sound provides reinforcement. The assistant watches the recipient's chest, making the chosen sounds exactly as the recipient exhales. As the session proceeds, the recipient only listens, but by hearing the expected words or sounds is able to sustain a focus that would otherwise be disturbed by a stream of thoughts.

When a patient is approaching death, comeditation is the ideal vehicle for nurturing the person's body, emotions, and spirit. As meditation serves as an aid in dealing with physical symptoms and myriad anxieties during day-to-day living, the meditative state is even more valuable during the dying process, when variations in body chemistry bring about additional and challenging physical and mental changes.

Because comeditation involves two people, the assistant may also experience calm and comforting, if he or she is in a relaxed position.

Richard Boerstler, 115 Blue Rock Road, South Yarmouth, MA 0664, USA (tel 001 508 394 6520).

Fasting to a "comfortable death"

'The art and science of fasting – Abstinence from food and drink as a means of accelerating death', a 28-page research paper by Chris Docker in the booklet Beyond Final Exit *(published by The Right to Die Society of Canada, PO Box 39018, Victoria, British Columbia, V8V 4X8; 1995, ISBN 1 896533 043; 14 American or Canadian dollars incl. p&p). Reviewed by Nicholas Albery.*

The Natural Death Centre has always argued, on balance, against active euthanasia (see the *Good Death* book review above, concerning the slippery slope danger); although the Centre recognises that there are very convincing arguments on both sides of the debate. At the same time, the Centre has supported the concept of passive euthanasia, particularly death by fasting. In the *Natural Death Handbook*, there were stories from the partners of two people who had peacefully fasted to death. The advantages seemed to include that the method was slow and relatively dignified and called for determination whilst allowing for second thoughts (rather than just popping some pills and pulling a plastic bag over one's head); that it was already legal to refuse force feeding either verbally at the time or in advance through one's living will; and that as a way of dying it would tend to be hard on the relatives – and therefore it was less likely that the patient would feel pressured to adopt it.

The *Natural Death Handbook* called for further reports on this under-researched topic, and this paper on 'The art and science of fasting' by Chris Docker is a truly admirable contribution to filling the gap. Chris Docker helps run the Voluntary Euthanasia Society in Scotland; he maintains an excellent Web site for the Society; and he remains patient and courteous with those on the other side of the debate. He is also an authority on living wills and points out in this paper that, in 20 out of 39 American states, the legislation in favour of living wills specifically excludes termination of life by the withdrawal of nourishment and hydration.

'A number of studies indicate fasting and even dehydration are not painful ways to go'

Whilst in his paper he comes to a different conclusion to that of the Natural Death Centre – for he believes that "fasting may be an uncertain course for an individual to embark on, especially when suitable drugs for self-deliverance can be obtained without too much difficulty in most countries and so provide an alternative route to dying in dignity" – and whilst he does not deal with the matter of whether or not a slow dying is preferable, he does report a number of reassuring medical studies which seem to indicate that, with doctors to assist where necessary, fasting and even dehydration are not painful ways to go.

The following are adapted extracts from the core of his paper:
Let us examine some of the evidence of peaceful and dignified deaths by fasting. While there are individual, anecdotal reports that seem to offer much hope, the two principle sets of data I propose to draw attention to cover:
   a) voluntary fasting by a particular religious sect and
   b) voluntary fasting in a hospital or, more usually, hospice setting.

With this second category will also be grouped withdrawal or nutrition and hydration in competent patients. These groups, however, may be considered to some extent atypical. The former covers an ascetic and well controlled graduated fast by relatively healthy subjects; the second relates primarily to subjects who are mostly elderly, terminally ill and, most importantly, have access to adequate palliative care.

'Voluntary fasting to death within a religious sub-group, the Terapantha order within the Jaina Digambara community in India'

Voluntary fasting to death within a religious sub-group appears to be confined to the Terapantha order within the Jaina Digambara community in India, where it is said that several well known cases occur every year.

The fast is described in Bioethics (Bilimoria P, 'A report from India: The Jaina ethic of voluntary death', Bioethics 1992; 6(4):331-355):

> In early 1983, a prominent Jaina scholar and writer by the name of Jinendra Varnî, then in his early eighties, although in reasonable health, decided that he wanted to fulfil his life's journey through a dignified yogic death (samadhimarana). On April 12th '83, Varnî formally withdrew from

his worldly commitments and upon request received from the head preceptor of his order, with due acclamation for his courage, initiation into the vow of terminal fast (sellekhana). He had already reduced his food intake; now as each day went past he cut back on certain vegetables, milk, clarified butter, yoghurt, dried fruits, giving up something every day, but retaining small portions of boiled vegetables and sultanas for one meal of the day.

'Varnî received initiation into the vow of terminal fast'

Occasionally he would fast all day long, and break the fast with broth from a boiled vegetable. By the end of the month his fluid intake was reduced as well and gradually given up, with plain water remaining as his only intake, which too was set aside on alternate fast days. On May 23rd, water was given up altogether. Varnî reclined with his body to one side during the last days, but there was apparently no evidence of hunger pangs, pain of any other kind (particularly from by-now deteriorating internal organs), barring some coughs and discomfort while sitting upright owing to his frail frame; nor did he show any significant loss of attention and consciousness. On May 24th, exuding a tremendous peace and calm in his general demeanour, Varnî closed over his eyelids and breathed his last.

This reassuringly peaceful death is a far cry from the horrors of starvation recounted elsewhere. Glimmerings that death from starvation and/or dehydration may not be as horrific as often contemplated have filtered through in mainstream medical literature for some time, probably starting with early fasting studies, through observations in palliative care when hospice workers realized that artificial nutrition and hydration were not necessarily beneficial to terminally ill cancer patients, and finally in recent years amidst the right to die debate, advocacy of willed fasting as a means to legal self-deliverance combined with the palliative assistance of hospice care.

In looking at comfort measures for the terminally ill, Billings went a stage further in noting: "... fluid depletion in dying patients should be regarded as a disorder with relatively benign symptoms. Successful treatment of the discomfort of thirst and a dry mouth generally does not require rehydration." By 1988, Printz had publicised the little-known situation where:

> ... A hospice nurse in 1983 noted a correlation between comfort and lack of medical hydration. It appeared to her that terminally ill patients in end-stage dehydration experienced less discomfort than patients receiving medical hydration. The dehydration, resulting from lack of nasogastric or IV fluid, seemed to produce a natural anaesthetic effect, often allowing for a reduction in pain medications.

A study by Andrews and Levine published in 1989 showed widespread support among hospice workers for dehydration in some terminal patients:

'53% of nurses agreed that dehydration can be beneficial for the dying'

Of the hospice nurses surveyed, 71 per cent agreed that dehydration reduces the incidence of vomiting, 73 per cent agreed that dehydrated patients rarely complain of thirst, 51 per cent reported that there is relief from choking and drowning sensations when fluids are discontinued, and 53 per cent agreed that dehydration can be beneficial for the dying patient. Also, 85 per cent of nurses surveyed disagreed with the need for hydration by IV and/ or tube feeding when dehydrated patients have a dry mouth. Finally, 82 per cent of the nurses disagreed with the statement that dehydration is painful.

They concluded that, in contrast to the assumption of most health professionals, dehydration was not painful, and that it was therefore a viable alternative to facilitate a comfortable death.

'The *only* method at the present time in which all sides in the "right to die" debate may reach common agreement under the law'

As death from lack of nutrition alone is a potentially very lengthy process, a combination of ceasing nutrition and hydration by some method is likely to be a preferred course. This area undoubtedly needs much more research. While a peaceful death by this method seems feasible in some instances, *without particularized medical advice and medical backup,* and/or until more is known about the process of self-deliverance through fasting, an isolated individual acting alone would appear to have greater assurance of success by means of drugs. Abstinence from food and drink as a means of accelerating death does however have the distinction of being the *only* method at the present time in which all sides in the 'right to die' debate may reach common agreement under the law.

Having tried to separate myth, misinformation and 'scare stories' from well-documented evidence, it is still difficult to say that refraining from food and drink will guarantee a peaceful death. Someone wanting a 100% foolproof method might consider it foolhardy to emulate Jinendra Varnî. A young, obese woman who has never followed a healthy diet might be ill-advised to attempt total fasting – even in the face of unrelievable distress or lingering, terminal illness.

But this is an area where a personal medical advisor may be able to narrow the odds and, if things go wrong, keep you comfortable in your dying without violating any laws and being branded a criminal.

This book can be obtained in the UK for £8 (incl. p&p) from The Voluntary

Creative Endings, £5-95 by credit card from The Natural Death Centre, tel London 0181 208 2853

Euthanasia Society of Scotland, 17 Hart Street, Edinburgh EH1 3RN (tel 0131 556 4404; fax 0131 557 4403; e-mail: <didmsnj@easynet.co.uk>; Web: <http://www.netlink.co.uk/users/vess/#links>).

Isn't starving to death cruel?

Adapted extract from an item in an unidentified Right-to-Die e-mail. The Right-to-Die e-mail group, which provides news on euthanasia issues, is contactable via <http://www.efn.org/~ergo/subscribe.html>.

"Isn't starving people to death cruel?" Persons in an irreversible coma or persistent vegetative state are in deep coma. They have no sense of time and they do not feel pleasure or pain. They do not sense the withdrawal of artificial nutrition and hydration.

'In a natural death, the terminally ill person refuses food and all but sips of water'

For all of history, until very recently, people have been dying without artificial nutrition and hydration. In a natural death, the terminally ill person does not want and even refuses food and all but sips of water.

It is natural for the dying to refrain from ingesting food and water. It is unnatural to "force-feed" the dying.

In 1986, Belding Scribner, MD, Professor of Medicine at the University of Washington, inventor of long term artificial kidney treatment and consultant on nutrition and hydration, testified before the Washington State Senate about whether it is humane to withdraw hydration.

He stated the following:

Withholding of hydration has to be considered in two parts: First, the withholding of salt water (normal saline) causes no pain and suffering of any kind. It takes weeks or months for significant salt depletion to develop and, when it does, the effect is a gradual drop in blood pressure and eventually a painless death from severe low blood pressure.

Secondly, concerning withholding of plain water, here is where opponents conjure up images of the '49ers dying of thirst in Death Valley with horrible thirst, swollen tongues and cracked lips. The case is quite different for the comatose, terminally ill patient lying in bed, usually in an air-conditioned environment.

The condition of the mouth depends upon the oral hygiene provided by the nursing staff, not on the state of hydration. Thirst, if present, is very subtle and easily treated, where appropriate, with ice chips or sips of water. There is no other pain and suffering that occurs.

Australian territory legalises euthanasia

Whilst recognising the courage and good faith of the voluntary euthanasia protagonists and the fine balance in the arguments, the Natural Death Centre has tended to argue in favour of passive euthanasia (the right to refuse force feeding, etc) and against active euthanasia. The first law permitting voluntary euthanasia, however, took effect, at least briefly, in Australia's Northern Territory from July 1st '96, but was under immediately under challenge in the Supreme Court from the Australian Medical Association and an aboriginal group. A bill in the federal parliament was also mooted to strip the Northern Territory of the power to allow termination of life. The following is extracted from an Associated Press report carried in the London Times.

Fred Finch, the Health Services Minister, warned terminally ill Australians not to rush to the Northern Territory to end their lives.

"It is important that people understand the strict conditions of legislation and do not simply uproot themselves from their homes and families to travel to the territory with false expectations," he said.

The voluntary euthanasia bill was passed in the Northern Territory parliament in May '96 and took effect on July 1st '96. Mr Finch said education programmes required by the law had been put into place. All medical practitioners and nurses in the Northern Territory will be invited to attend the programmes.

A public education campaign will include a euthanasia advice free telephone hotline and brochures explaining the workings of the Act.

A group was expected to begin developing an aboriginal education programme. Aborigines had opposed the bill, some being afraid that if they sought medical treatment they would be killed.

'A terminally ill patient must be evaluated by a psychiatrist to make sure her or she is not depressed'

The law requires that a terminally ill patient seeking to die must be evaluated by a psychiatrist to make sure her or she is not depressed. Euthanasia would be administered by a lethal overdose of drugs under medical supervision. Australia's immigration laws would bar terminally ill foreigners from going to the territory to end their lives. However, Australians from other states in the country could travel there.

The Bill makes the Northern Territory the first government to legalise voluntary euthanasia.

Doctors in the Netherlands may perform mercy killings within strict legal guidelines, but euthanasia is technically illegal. In America, Oregon voters approved a law allowing assisted suicide in 1995, but an injunction blocked it from taking effect pending a judge's ruling.

Death awareness leads to moral extremism

Michael Kearl

The following unexpected conclusions come from an Internet Web page on the Sociology of Death and Dying, written by Michael Kearl and located at <http://WWW.Trinity.Edu/~mkeral/death.html#di>.

Huntington and Metcalf observed in *Celebrations of Death*, "life becomes transparent against the background of death". In a way analogous to the experimental method of subatomic physicists, bombarding and shattering the nuclei of atoms in order to reveal their constituent parts and processes, death similarly reveals the most central social processes and cultural values. Death is a catalyst that, when put into contact with any cultural order, precipitates out the central beliefs and concerns of a people.

'When awareness of death is increased, prejudice and religious extremism escalate'

Abram Rosenblatt et al found, for example, that when reminded of their mortality, people react more harshly toward moral transgressors and become more favourably disposed toward those who uphold their values. In one experiment, 22 municipal judges were given a battery of psychological tests. In the experimental group, 11 judges were told to write about their own death, including what happens physically and what emotions are evoked when thinking about it. When asked to set bond for a prostitute on the basis of a case brief, those who had thought about their death set an average bond of $455, while the average in the control group was $50. The authors concluded that when awareness of death is increased, in-group solidarity is intensified, out-groups become more despised, and prejudice and religious extremism escalate.

American murder statistics

Another surprising titbit from Kearl's death-related Web pages.

Between 1976 and 1993, more Americans were murdered in their native land than died on the battlefields of World War II.

Michael C. Kearl, Department of Sociology and Anthropology, Trinity University, 715 Stadium Drive, San Antonio, Texas 78212 (e-mail: <mkerl@trinity.edu>).

How to avoid misdiagnosing death

Adapted extracts from an article by Dr Luisa Dillner in the Guardian entitled 'The last wrongs', monitored for the Natural Death Centre by Yvonne Malik.

Misdiagnosing death may seem like the ultimate in incompetence, but most doctors can see how it very occasionally happens. There is supposedly a standard procedure for pronouncing death, but few medical schools teach it formally. Looking thorough a selection of manuals for house officers, the main pronouncers of death in most hospitals, reveals a curious non-uniformity of advice.

Some advocate listening to the heart and lungs with a stethoscope for one minute – the absence of both being highly suggestive of death. But other manuals suggest three minutes, while a textbook on forensic medicine advises listening for five. It warns that people who are still hanging in there may only breathe once every 30 seconds, and have 12 feeble heart beats a minute.

> 'Most manuals advise doctors to feel for the carotid pulse (at the side of the neck) and to shine a light in the eyes'

Most manuals advise doctors to feel for the carotid pulse (at the side of the neck) and to shine a light in the eyes. The pupils of the dead do not react and stay dilated. There is a more sophisticated sign called 'rail-roading' where the blood in the eye breaks up into clumps, but no one I know has seen it.

Most doctors know that a profound coma can simulate death, particularly one induced by an overdose of barbiturates, which causes the body's temperature to drop and depresses the heart and respiratory rate.

Terminally ill patients, on high doses of morphine, can also be almost but not completely dead for a while.

In the light of recent mistakes, doctors may move towards the presumption that whoever they are called to see is alive unless there's strong evidence to the contrary. Blackwell's *Handbook For Housemen* cautions that: "sixty seconds can seem an awfully long time when listening to a manifestly dead patient's heart and lungs. However, it is not good practice to cut corners in this situation."

Lower life insurance for agreeing to sell one's organs

Robin Hanson

The following is an adapted extract from an e-mail message to the Alternative Institutions discussion group on the Internet (to subscribe to this online discussion group, send a request to: <AltInst-request@cco.caltech.edu> and wait up to two business days). For the full text and debate, see <http://hss.caltech.edu/~hanson/altinst-archive>.

There are some things that many folks don't think ordinary people should be allowed to buy or sell, but that they don't seem to mind letting insurance companies do. So you can't let people bet on when other folks might die, unless they're an insurance company.

Here is another example of this concept. A paper by Henry Hansmann, entitled 'The Economics and ethics of markets for human organs' (Journal of Health Politics, Policy and Law, 14:57, 1989) proposes that people be allowed, when signing their life insurance contracts, to agree to give up their organs when they die. Upon death, the insurance company could then sell those organs to those with medical needs for them. Anticipating these sales, the insurance company would offer lower premiums to those who agree to this.

This scheme should improve the supply of organs while avoiding those scenarios people worry about, of poor folks selling their kidneys for cash.

Robin Hanson, 2433 Oswego Street, Pasadena, CA 91107, USA (tel 001 818 683 9153; fax 001 818 405 9841; e-mail: <hanson@hss.caltech.edu>). His collection of online ideas is traceable via: <http://hss.caltech.edu/~hanson/home.html#AboutMe>.

AFTER DEATH

The Dead Citizens Charter

Comments by the Natural Death Centre

The Dead Citizens Charter, launched in draft form by the National Funerals College, aims to improve the way funerals are handled. The charter is perhaps unfortunately named, since the dead person has few rights, beyond the right for the body to be treated with dignity and the right to be remembered for his or her qualities during life. The rights that the College enumerates are mainly those of the next-of-kin or of those looking after the funeral arrangements. The charter should be renamed the Funerals Charter.

It should also be given more teeth and more specificity. If a right is worded as waffle and generalities, it will be ignored. The fact that the funeral trade seems minded to accept the charter's draft list of rights, whilst objecting vehemently to the more radical code being drawn up by the Institute of Burial and Cremation Authorities, suggests that this Dead Citizens Charter may be something of a missed opportunity – unless it does indeed take on board comments received and succeed in tightening up the final version.

Creative Endings, £5-95 by credit card from The Natural Death Centre, tel London 0181 208 2853

'People should have the right to arrange a funeral without a funeral director'

There are 24 rights listed in the charter. Some of these are excellent and do suggest improvements on present practice. For instance, there is:
- The right to arrange a funeral without the services of a funeral director.
- The right to a funeral service that recounts the life and the death of the person, recognising their uniqueness and the relationships that death has broken.
- The right to choose, subject to statutory health and safety restrictions, whether or not the body should be embalmed.
- The right to choose what happens to the body before the funeral. This includes the right to choose whether it should lie at home; what clothes are to be worn for the laying out and funeral (subject to statutory restrictions); whether the coffin is to be left open and its closure witnessed; and whether the body should rest overnight in a church or in any other place where the funeral service is to be held next day.
- The right to expect that the person, religious or secular, who is conducting the funeral, will contact and speak with the family beforehand.
- The right to a wider range of memorials.

What is missing?

What is missing from the list of rights in the draft charter? Very specific minimum standards should, the Natural Death Centre believes, be explicitly detailed in the summary of rights, not hidden in the body of text, as the public will hardly ever see the full document. What else could be added to the list of rights to help to improve funerals in future?

In the Natural Death Centre's opinion, the following would help:
- The right of the next-of-kin to visit the body, whatever advice they may receive to the contrary.

[Visiting the body includes the right to see *and* touch. The traumatised mother, for instance, refused the right to see and touch the body of the son who died in a motorbike accident, because it was felt that it would unnecessarily distress her, is only further traumatised and left with longer term resentments.]

- The right, recognised by law, but sometimes obstructed by hospitals in practice, for the next-of-kin rather than a funeral director, to be given the body of the deceased by a hospital, if no funeral director is being used.

[The Natural Death Centre, on several occasions, has had to send faxes to hospitals reminding them that the next-of-kin are legally entitled to possession of the body.]

- The right for the body to remain undisturbed for a period after death, if so desired by the next-of-kin, for religious or other reasons.

[For Tibetan Buddhists and others, it is considered necessary to leave the body undisturbed for up to three days.]
- The right to obtain information leaflets – on free funerals, inexpensive funerals and funerals without funeral directors – from hospitals, registrars, citizens advice bureaux, social security offices, crematoria and cemeteries.
- The right of funeral suppliers, crematoria and cemeteries to sell cardboard and other coffins to members of the public direct, without receiving threats from funeral directors.

[The Natural Death Centre knows of a number of instances where coffins had to be withdrawn from sale following threats from funeral directors. The Office of Fair Trading is currently looking into this abuse.]
- The right of the public to obtain a funeral through their local authority (or a simple body disposal service, for those who feel that this is all they require).

'For some people, a "body disposal service" should be on offer'

[Every local authority should contribute to keeping funeral prices down, by making available a cheap basic funeral, as the best now do. However, many correspondents to the Natural Death Centre go beyond this, wanting their body to be disposed of simply, cheaply and without any ceremony at their death – and for such people, a 'body disposal service' should be on offer.]
- The right for the body to be given back to nature after death, if so desired, and therefore, the right of the public to be offered Green funeral options, thus requiring every local authority to make available a Green or woodland burial ground, where a tree is planted instead of having a headstone; and requiring every funeral director to make available cardboard coffins, shrouds or similar biodegradable body containers.
- The right to be buried or cremated in whatever body container is desired, subject to environmental and technical constraints, whether this be a shroud or a cardboard coffin or a willow coffin or alternative container.

[Shrouds are normally stiffened with an inner plank, then lowered into the grave with attached ropes.]

'People should be able get a breakdown of prices over the telephone and through leaflets on display'

- The right of the public to purchase assistance from funeral directors on an à la carte basis, rather than having to buy a complete package.

[If a family wants just a coffin, body transport, refrigeration, hearse or bearers, they should be able to obtain a particular aspect from the funeral director, without paying for a complete package.]
- The right to obtain a fully itemised breakdown of the funeral director's prices

over the telephone and through leaflets on display in funeral directors' premises.
[In the States, a 1984 funeral regulation ensures this. To choose the most suitable funeral director is hard enough at a time of stress, without funeral directors concealing the necessary information.]
• The right to a clear indication, on all leaflets, shop fronts and notepaper, as to whether a funeral director is part of a larger chain.
[This needs to be in the rights section of the charter. Too many chains try to hide behind shop-fronts that look as if they belong to a small family firm.]
• The right for the public to be informed of a 'basic funeral' option in all a funeral director's price leaflets and presentations.
[Many funeral directors, although obliged by their code of practice to offer a basic funeral, do their best to conceal its existence.]
• The right to a wider range of memorials, including the right to any inoffensive nicknames, verses or designs on memorials.
[This is more specific than the charter's 'right to a wider range of memorials'.]
• The right of every citizen to an obituary and to be remembered for his or her worthwhile qualities.
[In this age of cheap electronic information storage, it should be the right of every citizen to have an obituary published, whether on the Internet or elsewhere, as part of the basic funeral package, even for social security funerals. It could become part of the minister's or officiant's role to assist, when necessary, with the writing of this obituary, for a small fee.]

The Dead Citizens Charter is available for £5 (inc. p&p, with cheques payable to 'The Mutual Aid Centre') from the National Funerals College, Braddan House, High Street, Duddington, Stamford, Lincs PE9 3QE (tel 01780 444269; fax 01780 444586).

• *Readers are invited to send their suggested additional 'rights' to the Natural Death Centre (20 Heber Road, London NW2 6AA, tel 0181 208 2853; fax 0181 452 6434; e-mail: <rhino@dial.pipex.com>) and these will be copied for forwarding to the National Funerals College.*

Response

Michael Young, founder of the National Funeral College, replies:
Your points seem very fair to me and will be welcome.
Only I don't agree about the name Funerals Charter, it would sound like something from SCI [the American funeral giant, Service Corporation International – ed] or the industry generally. Dead Citizens Charter is of course a play on Citizens Charter but why not? Dead people have hundreds of rights in law, eg to control the inheritances and copyrights. The rights of the bereaved are generated by the death of a person.
Michael Young, Insitute of Community Studies, 18 Victoria Park Square, Bethnal Green, London W2 9PF (tel 0181 980 6263; fax 0181 981 6719).

Funeral directors still failing to obey their own code

The National Association of Funeral Directors, in its magazine Funeral Director (May '96), reports an extraordinarily high failure rate on the part of its members to obey the Association's code, despite repeated published pleas from the Association, condemnations in the *Natural Death Handbook*, *Which?* magazine, etc.

In 172 inspections of member firms during 1995, they found that

'32.5% of funeral directors failed to display a price list'

- 11 per cent failed to display the Association logo.
- 13.9% failed to have readily available a written price list.
- 15.7% failed to provide written confirmation of funeral arrangements.
- 8.7% failed to provide written estimates.
- 4.6% failed to provide a specification of a basic funeral.
- 32.5% failed to display a price list.
- 35.4% failed to display the Code of Practice Principles.

Members of the public are advised to beware of Association firms which fail in any of the above categories. Complaints can be made to the Association, although these do not seem to be always handled to the satisfaction of the public. But for real and substantial financial redress, where warranted, the most effective route may be to take out a small claim in your local county court for negligence or breach of contract.

National Association of Funeral Directors, 618 Warwick Road, Solihull, West Midlands B91 1AA (tel 0121 711 1343).

Funeral company's high pressure tactics

Adapted extract from an article entitled 'Have a nice death' by Peter Godwin and Sarah Boseley in the Guardian (Feb 27th '96)

Service Corporation International (SCI) is the biggest funeral company in the world, with a big stake in Canada, Australia, France – and it has now captured 15 per cent of the UK market.

The BBC TV Public Eye documentary programme (broadcast on Feb 27th '96) obtained some internal documents revealing SCI's corporate strategy for the

UK: to increase the average spend on funerals, acquire more funeral homes, promote more aggressive selling and expand their market share. SCI's Funeral directors are offered a strategy to overcome their "difficulty combining their helping role with that of a business role". When selling a coffin:

- Present the coffin range to its advantage.
- Direct the attention of the family to the highest quality item on display (perhaps the Regal).
- Next present the Crown.
- Then present the Classic Royal, and so on in descending price order.
- Do not judge the ability of a family to afford a particular coffin or casket by their appearance. Prejudging could mean you talk yourself out of a higher priced item and your selling technique will reflect this.

The memo suggests the salesman should remain in the selection room unless the family ask for privacy allowing him to stay in control of the selection procedure. It continues :

- Know how to respond to objections: respond with empathy not defensiveness or aggression or impatience. For example, "I can understand your concern about the price but let me explain the difference in design and manufacture, again." Or, for example, "Yes, I can see your point about them just going into the ground, but we need to provide an extensive range like this in order to suit everyone's taste."

SCI talks of offering new options to customers. In practice, this means selling a more expensive range of coffins and memorabilia than has been customary.

Common misconceptions within the funeral trade

John Bradfield, author of Green Burial *(published by the Natural Death Centre), spoke on the subject of green funerals, and on behalf of the A. B. Wildlife Trust, at the National Association of Funeral Directors conference in Edinburgh, on May 16th '96. The following is an adapted extract from his talk, the full text of which is due to be published by the Association or may be obtainable from the author.*

I have given this address the title of 'Would You Believe It?', because I did for many years – and now realise I should not have done. If I read anything about procedures around dying and death, when a hospital social worker and educator, I accepted it as true. If an expert said or did anything, I assumed they knew the law. Now I am very cautious – even to the point of not trusting so-called 'evidence' of the law, in case it has been taken out of context, is misleading or just plain wrong. I am now so wary, I no longer believe anything unless I have checked it for myself.

I want to draw your attention to the ubiquitous ignorance surrounding dying and death, which allows beliefs to pass as facts, whether plausible or absurd. Why we live with such an appalling level of ignorance is an area for study in its own right.

'It matters that most people have no understanding of death, because real choice is only possible with full and accurate information'

Does it matter if most people have no understanding of the subject? Does the level of misinformation being circulated really matter? It does, in that real choice is only possible with full and accurate information.

Training courses continue to neglect this area. Even in 1983, it was noted with dismay that those with social studies backgrounds, like myself, had a blind spot on the subject of the impacts of death and funerals. If health and social services staff pick up the phone to get advice on law from a senior colleague, there is every chance that no one will be able to help or, worse, the information given will be legally flawed. Even solicitors working in the health service and local government, admit that they do not know the law or, have all too often given wrong advice.

Before I turn to examples of misinformation, I need to clarify the meaning of 'green' in my subject, as printed in the Conference timetable. At its simplest, it is a very practical approach to living, which meets the needs of people, without jeopardising opportunities for future generations, or the natural world in all its forms.

'Raise one hand, if you sell any products made of mahogany'

To give a very tangible example of the link between the needs of people and wildlife, I would be grateful if you could raise one hand, and keep it up, if you sell any products made of mahogany, whether as solid wood or veneer...

[Estimate of percentage of hands raised: about 50% to 60%.]

People living in rainforests continue to be killed by men employed by logging companies, trying to get mahogany for you to sell. This is encapsulated in the Friends of the Earth slogan 'Mahogany is Murder'.

In various parts of Africa, "logging companies, mostly from Western Europe, are pushing into the remaining forest areas" and workers have been killing gorillas and other apes for food, pushing them closer to extinction (Greg Neale, Sunday Telegraph, 14.4.96: 36). The murder of forest peoples and wild animals, has been the invisible price we have been paying for tropical timbers. What was invisible is now visible and we can use the money in our pockets to support or protest.

Now you are aware of these atrocities, if you were not already aware, how many of you will continue to sell mahogany and other timbers from tropical forests?

I know this is embarrassing ...
[Estimate of percentage of hands raised: about 50% to 60%.]

'One way of raising standards is to ask penetrating questions of manufacturers and suppliers, including the "environmentally-friendly"'

One way of raising standards, to put your firm head and shoulders above the rest in your area, is to ask penetrating questions of manufacturers and suppliers, including those which claim their products are environmentally-friendly. Such claims are, according to the National Centre for Toxic & Persistent Substances, "often misleading and not substantiated by technical data".

I urge to develop this discussion and a code of practice.

One of the oldest beliefs of all, which remains common even today, is that fees have to be paid for taking bodies over county boundaries. A Macmillan Nurse in a London hospice recently cautioned a widow about the complexity and costs of taking her husband's body up to Northumberland. She wasted time, money and emotional energy, ringing around for details of the law. Finally, she contacted the AB Wildlife Trust Fund, only to discover no such fees have ever existed.

Another common myth is that the law has required the use of coffins for transporting bodied to funerals and/or for burials. Your own Simon Truelove [ex-public relations officer for the National Association of Funeral Directors] states in the May 1994 edition of your journal, Funeral Director, that the Church of England had recently relaxed its laws, to permit uncoffined burials. Many undertakers I have met still insist that coffins must be used for burials, which suggests that they have never arranged a Muslim funeral or have provided a disservice – in that Muslims do not use coffins by choice.

'No law has ever required the use of coffins in any type of burial place'

It should be well known to you and your colleagues that no law has ever required the use of coffins in any type of burial place. This being so, you have a vital role to play in pointing out to local councillors and public cemetery staff, that any local rules about using coffins are negotiable. More significantly, it can be argued that the 'Race' Relations Act 1976 implicitly requires that Muslims be able to follow their own traditions, by not using coffins. As no majority or minority community has any special privileges in law, the same option must be available to anyone.

Do you advise, or *direct* on funerals?

I will never forget the words of a very well organised man, who arranged a burial in a nature reserve. He was worried the funeral would be stopped, if I did not hand the 'green form' to the undertaker, who had been asked to provide transport on the day. This message had been given by the undertaker and it is one printed in many texts. It is misleading, in that a burial authorisation must exist, as the small print states on the form, but it must be given to the landowner, manager or person who 'keeps' the land burial register. I was that person in this case.

During the funeral, this very capable man kept asking the undertaker if he would mind if the family did certain things, which they had planned together. Rather than say he was there to be used by the family as it saw fit, an atmosphere of nonchalance and tension existed until the family was alone. Then they became real again, as they rolled up their sleeves to create a burial mound, with their chosen music playing in the background.

John Bradfield, the A. B. Wildlife Trust, 7 Knox Road, Harrogate, North Yorkshire HG1 3EF (tel 01423 530900).

The greening of a cemetery
Ken West

The Carlisle Cemetery, managed by Ken West, and winner of the Natural Death Handbook award in 1993 for the most helpful cemetery in the UK, takes its responsibility for the environment very seriously. The following is adapted from a leaflet the Cemetery issued in February '96, outlining some of the issues. Their approach could certainly act as a model to less enlightened cemeteries.

Conservation areas. In 1992, Wards 1 and 2 of Carlisle Cemetery were designated as conservation zones. The grass in these areas is mown once each year in October. Reciprocating mowers are used, cutting the grass as if it were hay, and this is raked off and sent to the composting centre. Many wild flowers appeared including pignut, primrose, ox-eye daisy, knapweed and, in 1995, a single cowslip. In 1995, Meadow Brown butterflies and Burnett moths first appeared, and many insects are now evident. Each Summer, Spotted Flycatchers nest and feed in these areas. Unusually, some favourite Victorian plants have flourished. These include the wild daffodil and Dog-Tooth Violet. In these and other areas, bird and bat boxes have been created.

Herbaceous beds. Most beds have been replanted with species favoured by butterflies.

Owls. Residents of Richardson Street have recorded how the owls in the cemetery were regularly heard in the 1950s. They have since declined in number and species, and it is proposed to reverse this trend. Initially, the conservation areas will increase vole numbers, the main prey of owls. Owl boxes are being erected and access given to the roof-space in an old chapel.

Carved Owl. Artist Linda Watson carved a Barn owl from the trunk of an old Sweet Chestnut. 'Barnie' sits on Ward 3 looking over the conservation area, watching for voles no doubt! She has also carved an 'oak leaf' seat for the woodland grave site.

The Beck. The Fairy beck runs through the cemetery. Over the years it was straightened, with the banks mown by nymo type machines. This ceased in 1995, and dogrose, hazel and dogwood were planted along the banks in 1996. These are to provide cover for ducks and bank voles. In 1995, a kingfisher was observed on the beck, suggesting that the environment was improving. To help this species, three waterfalls were created in Spring 1996. These will form small pools able to sustain fish and amphibians.

Herons. Herons have nested in the cemetery for some years. We avoid disturbing them during the nesting period. Sadly, the poor Spring weather in recent years has killed some of the young birds.

'A feeding hopper for red squirrels has been erected in the cemetery'

Red Alert. The council are supporting projects to conserve the red squirrel. As red squirrels appear in the cemetery on occasion, a feeding hopper has been erected. This cannot be accessed by the heavier grey squirrel. The woodland burial area is also proposed as a future reserve for red squirrels.

Hedgehogs. Hedgehogs are safe in the cemetery. To help them hibernate, felled trees and timber are placed in 'habitat' piles, under which they can also nest. A local resident also rescues hedgehogs and, after recovery, these are released in the cemetery. We do not use poisons or slug bait in the cemetery, chemicals which can kill these creatures.

Memorials. The memorials in the cemetery date from 1855 to the current time. They are an important social record, as well as an essential substrate for lichens (see below). Unsafe memorials are never removed, except where a repair or sinking deeper in the ground is not possible. Modern memorials are made of foreign stone and the beautiful local sandstones are rarely used. Only a few stones each year are hand carved, most being produced by computer controlled sand blasting. The development of local sculptors using local stone would be worth promoting.

Lichens. These small plants are composed of a fungus and an algae, and look beautiful under a hand lens. They are disappearing throughout Europe, but grow moderately well in the clean air of Carlisle. Lichens grow on soil, trees and memorials. It is important that memorials are not moved, as the lichens often die in new positions.

Animal vandals. The cemetery sustains wildlife in surprising ways, some of which lead to complaints! Rabbits routinely eat the flowers neatly around the edge of wreaths left at funerals. They also nip off 'pot mums' leaving a neat stub. This leaves the plant looking as if a gardener had clipped the plant with a pair of shears. Carrion crows pull flowers out of vases in order to drink water. The holly berries on Christmas wreaths are also enjoyed by birds. What they think of the plastic berries, it is difficult to know!

Creative Endings, £5-95 by credit card from *The Natural Death Centre*, tel London 0181 208 2853

Woodland burial. This is the burial option used by those who are concerned with the environment. The graves will create a new oak forest, and, with the planting of Scots Pine, will create a squirrel reserve. Request a free leaflet if you require details.

Recycled grave. This option was developed following requests by those concerned about the wastage of land for burial. It is also the least expensive form of burial. These graves are owned by the council and situated in old, often very attractive parts of the cemetery. They have been used for two burials which occurred over 100 years ago. The remains of these burials have now disappeared into the soil. These graves are only suitable for single burials, and, not being 'private', a memorial cannot be placed. A biodegradable coffin must be used and the grave will be re-used for burial, some 75 to a 100 years from now. Further details are available.

Environmental cremation. A reduced cremation fee now applies if cremation is arranged using an inexpensive biodegradable coffin. The cremation will be completed on the same day as the service occurs, or the following morning. Please ask for further details if you are interested.

Biodegradable coffins. The standard coffin used today is made of chipboard and plastics. These cause pollution when cremated and the materials will not degrade into the earth after burial. A selection of biodegradable coffins, some made of recycled floorboards, and a wool burial shroud, can be seen in the old burial chapel. Please ask for details and free leaflets.

Recycling old wreaths. A recycling scheme for old wreath frames was introduced in Autumn 1995. The wreaths are collected from cemetery tip sites by a special needs group. They strip off the old flowers and these are sent for composting. The old frames and plastic trays, etc, are them sold back to the florists for reuse. The scheme has not been totally successful due to adverse criticism from the National Association of Funeral Directors.

Cemetery walks. Cemetery walks occur during the Spring and Summer. Contact us for current details, or see the East Cumbria Countryside Project walks leaflet.

Ken West, Bereavement Services, Cemetery Office, Richardson St, Carlisle, Cumbria CA2 6AL (tel 01228 25022).

Death – a return to the sacred grove

Erik van Lennep

In the UK, there is an Association of Nature Reserve Burial Grounds that networks the 25 or so woodland burial grounds where a tree is planted instead of having a headstone. In the following American article, originally published in Catalyst, Vol VIII, No. 3 and 4, and in Green Egg, and e-mailed to the Institute, Erik van Lennep imagines how such a movement might be in the States.

Memorial Day dawns with the soft light of late May, as a gentle breeze stirs the leaves of a richly varied forest canopy. As the Sun warms the Earth, birds are busily searching out food for Spring hatchlings, bees work the blossoms on a wealth of different species, and a tardy few deer return to their deep woods shelter after a night of browsing and carousing.

Hours later, humans begin to arrive for a day of reflection, reunion, and celebration among the groves. An elderly woman comes to plant hepaticas at the base of a young white oak. Tucking the roots into the dark compost amongst the oak's roots, she lovingly waters them, all the while talking to her husband, to the tree. They have been one in her mind since she planted the tree on his grave fifteen years ago.

Further down the slope a young family sits at the base of a grand chestnut, amidst a scattering of smaller chestnut trees – all blight resistant American chestnut cultivars, of course – and tells stories about the relatives and ancestors whose bodies now feed the trees where they have spread their blankets. In a ravine, stand great white pines planted to hold the banks against erosion after the last-ever clearcut on this site. Flying squirrels peak from nest cavities in the boles of the eldest trees.

Further upslope, a stand of shagbark hickories unfurls its leaflets like a bronzy green haze amidst the stout twiggy branches. The sounds of singing and the rasp of shovels against soil can be heard from the edge of the meadow, where a family in mourning is laying to rest the eldest of their Great Aunts, soon to be memorialized by a new thicket of her favourite wild plums. As a sign at the entrance reads, "We are all but compost for future lives. The cycle alone endures".

'The future sacred grove will be created by concern for damaged lands, climate stabilisation, increased old growth habitat, and new recreation lands'

This is a scene from the future sacred grove, created by a combination of concern for restoration of damaged lands, climate stabilisation, planning for the provision of increased old growth habitat, and creation of new recreation lands to alleviate pressure on vital wilderness. The land may have been secured through a new concept in land trusts, a trust devoted to environmental rehabilitation, and reclaimed through the hands of local citizens sick and tired of watching the world fall apart around them. A rehabilitation-as-empowerment project designed for and by youth may have played a key part. Sales of native plants, researched and cultivated by the youth eco-restoration corps not only helped to fund the cost of initial salvage operations, but continues today as a revenue source for the minimal management costs of the groves.

The community surrounding the groves also reflects the local nursery activity, in some areas having merged with the Forest of The Ancestors. Initial costs of

---

Creative Endings, £5-95 by credit card from The Natural Death Centre, tel London 0181 208 2853

purchasing land was through sales of cemetery plots, at well below the going rate for the burial industry, but sufficient for project needs. The first 'clients' were a combination of those whose families could not afford the high cost of plots and fees within the established system, baby boom environmentalists looking ahead as they reached middle age, and a scattering of garden clubbers and wilderness buffs.

Western industrial culture holds few things sacred. It will tolerate few mysteries within its realm. For this reason, respect is also a rarity within contemporary Western society. As a whole, we do not respect our parents, our elders, our ancestors, or our children. We do not respect our waters, the land, the air, or Earth's natural cycles. We do not respect our neighbours, and we do not respect other races or cultures. We rarely even respect ourselves.

On of the few forces allowed to retain some mystery, and therefore able to command some respect, is death. We accord some measure of respect to our own dead, and to their resting places. As callously as developers may treat the burial sites of other peoples' ancestors, our own graveyards may come as close to sacred ground as any other place identified with our culture.

'Final resting places would be marked by trees. Discreet markers would help families find the burial sites'

In the eco-cemetery, the final resting places would be marked by trees, or thickets and groves. Discreet markers at the base of trees would help families find the burial sites, and serve to commemorate the dead, but the most visible memorial would be in the living trees. Metaphysically, metaphorically, chemically, and conceptually, the dead would live on as a tree, a grove, an entire forest dedicated in loving memory.

While the impetus for the creation of eco-cemeteries may be found in a combination of economic and environmental concerns, the benefits go far beyond. The use of 'sacred grove' as both an expression and as a concept is powerful. By connecting people with a positive image of the cycles of Life, the ensuing generations will grow to respect both forests and ancestors in a manner not seen for many western generations. The community and family ritual of tree tending, coupled with acceptance of the natural order within a forest destined to grow old, will engender different attitudes than the obsessive manipulation and manicuring of today's cemeteries. Human communities and all forests will benefit from the sacred groves, and the West just might begin to understand the ideas held sacred by other cultures.

Erik van Lennep, in 1990 PO Box 73, Strafford, VT 05072, USA (e-mail: <Erik.Vanlennep@Dartmouth.EDU>). The author has a second document on how to organise such a Grove project.

The newest green burial grounds

The Association for Nature Reserve Burial Grounds knows of 33 green burial grounds open as of July '96, with 6 more about to open and more than 30 at the planning stage. A bishop has said off the record that he expects almost all Christian funerals to be green burials by the year 2020.

A green burial is one where often a tree is planted instead of having a headstone. A green burial ground that wants to become a member of the Association must agree to:
- allow families to conduct the funeral themselves if they so wish, without using a funeral director, including helping fill the grave;
- to manage their site ecologically;
- to allow burial in a shroud or cardboard coffin;
- to meet a number of other criteria designed the protect the public.

The six most recent woodland burial grounds to come to the notice of the Association are:
- **Gerrards Cross**: The *Parkside woodland burial ground*, dotted with pines and oaks and surrounded by woodland, is a 2 acre site on top of a hill within the 8 acre Parkside cemetery (Windsor Road, Gerrards Cross, Bucks SL9 8SS, phone Ian Ritchens on 01753 662426), run by the South Bucks District Council. It costs £168-70 (including digging & tree; £297-40 to non-residents). The public can dig the grave and fill it if they wish.
- **Oxford**: an Oxford City Council green burial ground. £335 (including digging, double to non-residents), tree £50, bulbs £25. Contact Hugh Dawson, Cemetery Manager, The Lodge, Wolvercote Cemetery, Banbury Road, Oxford OX2 8EE (tel 01865 513962).
- **Hillingdon**: a local authority woodland burial ground, which opened April '96. A wildflower meadow now with trees, with West Drayton Cemetery to one side and public open space to the other. £545 (including digging). Families can help fill the grave but not dig the grave. Contact David Bryant, Civic Centre, Uxbridge, Middlesex UB8 1UW (tel 01895 250416).
- **St Asaph**, Denbighshire: A small sloping field, as a woodland burial site with two burials so far, just off the main cemetery by the church, "very rustic, natural and peaceful". £270 (incl. the digging and the tree, double for non-residents). Mrs Sylvia Jones, Denbighshire County Council, Fforddlas Depot, Fforddlas, Rhyl, Denbighshire LL18 2EL (tel 01824 706455).
- [*] Nr. **Manchester**. A 12 acre woodland burial ground at City Road, Ellenbrook (in Mosley Common), Worsley, Near Manchester M28 1BD (phone James Broome on 0161 790 1300). £650 (including digging – a tree and a flat memorial stone are extra). Families can help fill the grave and can do a token amount of digging. "The site looks across open fields, and is surrounded with trees."

- **Seaton, Devon**: A woodland burial area for 150 graves run by the East Devon District Council within the Seaton Cemetery, Colyford Road, Seaton, Devon (tel 01395 516551), managed by Mr Kane and Mr Chris Burchill, with an internment fee of £57, digging of grave extra.
- **Maldon, Essex**: A woodland glade burial ground, near the A 414, run by the Maldon District Council (Council Offices, Princes Road, Maldon, Essex CM9 5DL, tel 01621 875836). £383 (incl. digging and the tree, £693 for non-residents).

For an information pack on 'Inexpensive, Green, Family-Organised Funerals', please send 6 first class stamps or a cheque for £1-56 to: The Natural Death Centre, 20 Heber Road, London NW2 6AA (tel 0181 208 2853; fax 0181 452 6434; e-mail: <rhino@dial.pipex.com>).

The latest on planning permission for d-i-y burials

In May '96, a man in East Sussex won his appeal to the Department of the Environment against his local authority, who had turned down his application for a Certificate of Lawfulness to have two burials in his half acre garden.

This, combined with a number of other Certificates of Lawfulness and the successful appeal against refusal of planning permission by Ian Alcock in Aberdeenshire, who now has the right to a 'limited number' of burials, containable within an area on his farm of 50 metres by 50 metres, would suggest that the scope for burial on private land without planning permission remains as interpreted by the Natural Death Centre:

A 'limited' number of burials (family, friends, those living in the house) on private land do not require planning permission.

For the law on private land burial, see Green Burial *by John Bradfield, obtainable for £9-85 (incl. p&p) from The Natural Death Centre (address above).*

Burial in a Connemara blanket

Margaret Love

Adapted from a letter to the Natural Death Centre.

I recently buried my husband in the green burial ground at Oakfield Wood, near Wrabness in Essex.

My husband had always assumed that he would be cremated, as being the most efficient and least demanding-on-precious-space way of disposing of his body.

Indeed, we had both recently paid quite a large sum to join the Luxembourg cremation society following the recent opening of a crematorium here. However, I had always said that what I would most like for myself would be for my family and friends to dig a hole and pop me in and cover me over – but I thought this was perhaps too much to ask of people.

When Brian did die, regretfully in hospital but protected from its potential excesses by his living will and by me, and in the privacy of a private room where we could play his favourite music and do little things to make the place more 'ours', I found the last thing I was going to do was to hand him over to the professionals. I had heard about the Natural Death Centre some time ago – on the radio – and set my brother on to tracking you down. As it happened, my sister-in-law had also heard of you and actually had some information. And so I found my way to John Acton, the farmer who runs the Oakfield Wood burial ground.

When I telephoned John to make an appointment to visit, he suggested Hunnaball Funeral Services of Colchester as a firm who had buried people at the site before, and so I called them. I think this was quite important, as Mr Hunnaball warned me that the name Oakfield Wood belies the current nature of the site – the land was farmed until recently and it will be many years before it takes on the aspect of a wood. It was a cold, windy day when I visited and the area looked pretty barren, until you noticed the thousands of tiny trees already planted around the perimeter and the few deciduous saplings planted on some graves. Its saving grace was that there were skylarks singing, even on this cold day. So burying your loved one here is an act of faith in what it will become in the future – and in nurturing the skylarks of the present – and someone has to be in at the beginning!

'Brian was covered in a Connemara blanket while lying on a board. No coffin'

We did not dig the hole – John Acton did that – and Hunnaballs fetched Brian from the Royal Marsden hospital. They also picked up the Connemara blanket from the Irish shop in London which I had ordered over the phone, and in which Brian was to be covered while lying on a board. No coffin. We helped carry Brian to the grave-side. I said a few words and read a poem, and then we helped the undertakers lower him into the grave. We then had more poems and some people spoke of Brian. And then we all filled in the grave. Very nice for John! The skylarks were still singing.

When we left I felt almost elated. I had asked a lot of the few members of our family and friends who were invited, and I think they were a bit nervous of the whole affair – no easy distancing from what is going on – but they all found it good and right and rather special.

Afterwards, we went to eat at the Stour Bay Café in Manningtree, which was rather special too. I had spoken to the proprietress over the phone and explained why we were coming and what we would have been doing, and that we might be muddy, and I didn't know just when we would arrive because I didn't know how long it took to fill in a grave. She said she didn't mind, and that they would wait until we got there, and she cooked us a wonderful meal and we drank some great wines.

So, that's nearly the end of the story except that it was Brian's birthday soon after I returned to Luxembourg and I used it to celebrate his life. Many friends came to eat, drink, reminisce, read poems, laugh, and cry only a little.

All this has helped me to gently close the door on that part of my life – 37 years of marriage – and open the door to whatever comes next.

Margaret Love, 8 Rue de L'Ernz, L-6196 Eisenborn, G. D. Luxembourg.

A family-organised funeral
Judith Furner

Adapted from a letter to the Natural Death Centre.

In 1984 my sister Lynn was diagnosed with ovarian cancer. She was operated on, had chemotherapy treatment and apparently recovered. Five years later she had cancer again, and once again was treated, apparently successfully. However, the cancer eventually returned, and in December 1994 we were told that she had only weeks to live. I found the hardest thing was accepting that she was going to die. Once I had accepted it, I found that I could cope with the process of her dying.

We lived in towns 20 miles apart, so I was able to visit her frequently, and in the last two or three weeks, I visited her daily. I found that the more I visited her, the more I came to terms with her dying, felt able to have the conversations that I needed, and, paradoxically, felt less anxious and miserable about the situation. Lynn wanted to be at home as much as possible, where she was cared for by Dave, her husband, her three adult daughters, two of whom moved in, and nurses provided by the Health Authority, such as district nurses and palliative care nurses. She was in some discomfort, but in no actual pain, which was controlled by drugs.

She spent a fortnight in a hospice after Christmas, but then said that she wanted to stay at home. Her health was deteriorating all the while, she was unable to keep food down, and eventually stopped eating altogether. A few days before she died, she said to me, I don't think it will be long now, and I hope it's not. She was tired of the discomfort and the weakness, and her spiritual beliefs enabled her to regard death as the last great adventure.

Lynn died peacefully at home on February 11th '95, with her family around her. My husband, Chris, and I arrived soon afterwards, as did my son Ben. We all sat on her bed with her body, talking quietly to each other and weeping a little. The district nurse telephoned the doctor, who arrived fairly soon to certify the death. Lynn had already said that she wanted a do-it-yourself funeral and green burial, and some arrangements had been made.

We told the nurse that we didn't want a funeral director, but she telephoned the Co-op on our behalf, and said that if at any point we couldn't cope, the Co-op was prepared to move in and take over. Although we knew in general what we wanted, I for one found some of the practicalities quite daunting.

'Lynn's daughters and Dave washed her body, cut her nails, brushed her hair and dressed her'

We wanted to keep Lynn's body at home, and the district nurse told us that we could only do that if she was embalmed because the process of decay would start. We thought that embalming would prevent her being biodegradable, so reluctantly we agreed that her body should go to the mortuary, so that it could be refrigerated and remain in a good state for anyone to visit before the funeral. Lynn's husband, Dave, went to the municipal cemetery, where there is a woodland burial ground, and a burial plot had already been arranged. He returned with a cardboard coffin, and we proceeded to prepare Lynn's body.

'We had some difficulty getting the coffin down the stairs. When the coffin was in the hall, we opened a bottle of champagne'

The district nurse had already removed the catheter and syringe driver, which had been supplying Lynn with an anti-nausea drug as well as a painkiller. We were aware shortly after her death that her body was stiffening, and we found it rather disconcerting as we had thought that it would take several hours. Lynn's daughters and Dave washed her body, cut her nails, brushed her hair and dressed her in a beautiful white cotton nightie which my mother had bought for her. Lynn's youngest daughter said, "She looks so beautiful, just like an angel", and indeed she did. We lined the coffin with a blue blanket, and put in a little lavender pillow that Lynn had used. We lifted her body into the coffin on the sheet she had been lying on. We had some difficulty getting the coffin down the stairs, and left the lid off so that we could be sure that her body was securely in place. When the coffin was in the hall we stopped dealing with the practicalities, and opened a bottle of champagne. We toasted Lynn, and bade her farewell. The three men of the family put the lid on the coffin, carried it out to their estate car, and drove it up to the cemetery mortuary to await the funeral.

Lynn and Dave had planned the funeral in detail. Lynn wanted it to be as personal as possible, with responsibilities carried out by the family rather than a funeral director. The only instance in which we deviated from her wishes was in using a hearse rather than the family estate car to take the coffin to the chapel from the mortuary, and then on to the burial ground. The municipal cemetery in Brighton, where Lynn was buried, has facilities for non-Christian ceremonies in the chapel, and Dave was encouraged to take advantage of this. The funeral was at 2pm, and we arrived at Dave's house at midday. We found a huge gathering with friends, family, alcohol already being consumed, and masses of flowers. We arrived at the chapel in good time. It was packed, there must have been a hundred people there. Lynn had chosen the music she wanted, and it was played while her coffin was carried in by Dave, Lynn's son-in-law, my brother and my husband.

Dave addressed us, and spoke of Lynn's life, and death, and what she had wanted at her funeral. He asked anyone who would like to, to stand up and speak about Lynn. Several members of the family, including myself and my brother and sister, did so. Friends from over the years, some of whom I did not even know, also spoke. It was an extremely moving ceremony, and each person who spoke clearly did so from the heart. Lynn was a wonderful person, and well-loved, and at her funeral we all came to appreciate her a little more. Dave then read a piece from the Bhagavadgita which he said he and Lynn had read together when they were first told that she had not long to live, and which had comforted them.

After the ceremony, the coffin was carried out to the hearse, and driven to the grave. Two undertakers assisted in lowering the coffin into the grave. My brother spoke words from the book of Common Prayer, including "ashes to ashes, dust to dust". He and Dave and the grave-digger remained at the grave to fill it in, while the rest of us returned to the house. Delicious food and plenty of wine was provided, and rather extraordinarily we had a party which went on for several hours. Several friends have subsequently told me that Lynn's funeral was the best funeral they had ever attended.

'Assisting with the preparation of the body and taking part in a true farewell at the funeral, is a very healing process'

It is a sad and terrible thing to lose a sister, but being close to everything that is going on, assisting with the preparation of the body and taking part in a true farewell at the funeral, is a very healing process.

Judith Furner, 11 St Helena Court, Eastbourne BN21 2LY.

Editorial comment

Normally it is in fact possible to keep the body at home, without embalming, at least for a few days. It may be advisable to turn off the heating in the room, open the window, and even, if necessary, use bags of ice or dry ice. The Natural Death Centre would like to be able to tell people where they can buy or rent a refrigeration plate such as that put under the body at home in French villages, should any reader know – or be able to manufacture and market these.

The Natural Death Centre, 20 Heber Road, London NW2 6AA (tel 0181 208 2853; fax 0181 452 6434; e-mail <rhino@dial.pipex.com>).

The dead good funeral

The Dead Good Funerals Book *by Sue Gill and John Fox (published by Engineers of the Imagination, Welfare State International, The Ellers, Ulverstone, Cumbria LA12 OAA, tel 01229 581127, ISBN 0 9527159 0 2, 192 pages) is available from the Natural Death Centre, 20 Heber Road, London NW2 6AA (tel 0181 208 2853 for credit card orders) for £11 incl. p&p. Nicholas Albery writes:*

Reading this book is like having a theatre director of great flair and genius at my shoulder, giving me tips about how to ginger up my own more conventional and timid ideas. It also contains a section of step-by-step information on what to do after a death, written up in a very wise and sensitive way by Ken West, manager of the Carlisle woodland burial ground and the pioneer of green burial in the UK – he has a great appreciation for the diversity of people's needs.

The Natural Death Centre, however, puts out a comment slip with each copy of this book that we send out, as there are, in the Centre's view, two minor amendments to be made, which are:

On page 11, the book says: "Graves must be dug to the required depth." In fact there is no law specifying the minimum depth of graves, although there may be a locally-relevant act or bye-law.

On page 49, the book says: "No planning approval is necessary [for a single burial, perhaps two burials, on private land]." Recent Certificate of Lawfulness council decisions go further than this and suggest that planning permission would not normally be required for a reasonable number of burials for family, friends and those living in the house.

But these are small niggles. To provide a taste of the book's breadth of vision, here are three adapted extracts, all on the theme of improving funerals.

A dozen ways to improve funeral arrangements at very short notice

• Think about where the funeral should be. It does not have to be in church (unless you want a C of E service). It could be for a small gathering at home, at a community centre, in the cricket pavilion, outside in a garden or woodland ...

• Think about whether you need a minister of religion or celebrant, or whether you have somebody who could lead the funeral ceremony. Make no mistake. This is a sensitive and difficult function. It must be someone experienced enough to maintain their composure throughout the proceedings.

• Pick up the telephone and speak to the manager of the crematorium or cemetery or a representative from any church or chapel you may be using. Tell them when you are coming for the funeral. Tell them if you have any particular requests.

• Decide if you would like extra time for the service for any reason and negotiate a suitable time of day. Ask about any extra charges.

- Find time to visit the place in advance and talk through with a member of staff what will happen when and where. Make sure you ask what the normal proceedings are (curtains close automatically? coffin glides away? coffin remains?) and be sure you are comfortable with this. Find out the limits of what is possible.
- Look at the artefacts displayed in the space (crucifix etc). If you do not want them, ask for them to be removed or covered up. Ask them to show you what lights are usually on.

> **'Candles, a special cloth or banner to drape the coffin, a lantern, decorations, a photograph in a frame'**

- Consider what you might bring in from home and talk to the manager about this. Candles, a special cloth or banner to drape the coffin, a lantern, decorations, a photograph in a frame, any characteristic personal object belonging to the person who has died. Who will bring it? When?

> **'In a modern crematorium the seats are not always fixed. Maybe a semicircle, or a circle would be good for a moderate size congregation'**

- How is the seating arranged? In a modern crematorium the seats are not always fixed, therefore there is no need for straight rows with everyone looking at each others' backs. Maybe a semicircle, or a circle would be good for a moderate size of congregation. If you request this, help the staff by agreeing to be the last funeral of the day, or the first.
- Do you want any music? The sound of the organ is inextricably linked for most of us with church services. Only book the resident organist if that is what you want. In some crematoria their services come free, and the use of the cassette player or CD player is charged for. In others, it is the other way round. You may prefer your own choice of prerecorded music. Check what playback facilities exist. For the entry/arrival it is usual to have 6-8 minutes of music, for the committal only a few bars are needed; exit music usually lasts about five minutes. Label each tape or CD clearly showing what is to be played when. Tapes should be set so your piece of music starts immediately it is switched on. Getting the music right is important. It is a good idea to make this the job of one person who will get there early. If you want no recorded music, you must say so, otherwise it could be switched on automatically as you arrive. If you want live music, find a musician (through music teachers in the yellow pages, music shops selling instruments, concert halls, music schools, amateur dramatic societies, or the Musicians' Union in London, tel 0171 582 5566).
- Think about individual contributions to the funeral service, such as one or two

people getting up to give an address, read a poem or tell a favourite story. Remember the film 'Four Weddings and a Funeral; and the powerful W H Auden poem 'Stop all the clocks'? Make definite arrangements that are clearly understood. Give a brief written running order to anyone involved. Avoid using microphones if you possibly can. If you must, then arrange a practice.

• If you would like to invite everyone to do something at the funeral, ie gather at the gate to walk together to the grave-side instead of driving, or throw a single flower into the grave, make sure you mention this clearly in the newspaper announcement. You will not have time to telephone everyone. It is possible for a few people to get practically involved after a burial by filling in the grave themselves, but only if you have requested this in advance, so they can supply enough shovels.

Discuss these plans with the cemetery or crematorium manager *and* your funeral director. The best and simplest thing you can do, in our opinion, is to *take the flowers out of the cellophane wrapping* for a start.

'Encourage everyone to bring along their photographs or souvenir albums to display'

• Consider some ideas for the gathering afterwards. You may encourage everyone to bring along their photographs or souvenir albums to display on a table for people to browse through together. This helps to break the ice and talk through memories of the person who has died, or build bridges between relatives whose lives have drifted apart. And don't be afraid to get out your camera or camcorder to record this get-together. This last scene of the family album is usually the one that is missing.

Suggested Structure for a Ceremony

Here is a suggested structure to follow for those wishing to organise a funeral ceremony that is both dignified and formal, yet simple:

• **Arrival and Welcome:** Opening words, including the name of the person whose life we are honouring. Mention and include the family or partners and their loss. The person (or preferably two) leading the ceremony may introduce themselves; outline their role; give an idea of the length of the ceremony; invite people to sit down and encourage people to move forward if it is a sparse gathering in a large venue; indicate anything particular that will happen during or after the ceremony.

• **Frame the Event:** Some action or gesture to mark the start of the ceremony, eg someone lights a candle or lantern near the coffin.

• **Set the Mood:** Listen to a piece of music; readings of verse and poetry with thoughts on the meaning and value of a life and the inevitability of death, chosen for their suitability to the person concerned (an old person dying at the end of a long and fulfilling life; a young adult killed in an accident; a child ...). The family may have suggested a favourite poem to be read. Everyone sings a secular song or a hymn together.

- **Tributes:**
To the life of .... given by friends, relatives, colleagues. Readings, stories, poems, or something a family member has written, to be read on their behalf. This can be an opportunity to quote from letters of condolence that have already come in.
- **Commital:** Invite people to stand; indicate it is time for the final part of the ceremony when we commit the body of .... to its natural end. Offer a short silence for people's own thoughts or prayers. If it is a crematorium, this is where curtains close or the coffin glides out of sight. At the grave-side this is the lowering of the coffin into the ground. A handful of earth, or flowers may be thrown into the grave.
- **Closing Words:** Focusing people back onto their own lives, moving forward, carrying this sorrow and loss. Thanks on behalf of the family to those attending and for recent support given, where appropriate. Final piece of music to listen to, or to sing together.
- **Depart for Social Gathering.**

Hanging the crem with banners and papercuts

John Fox describes the imaginary funeral of his imaginary twin brother, to give an example of how a creative funeral might be. (It started out as a proposal for his own funeral "but as I wrote it I realised I was being far too prescriptive. The dead can't control the living.")

Wrapped in his favourite blanket we placed his body in a deep blue shiny cardboard coffin painted inside and out. On the lid his daughter painted simple seed and tree designs in white lines. The coffin rested on trestles in the front room of his house for a day or two; we preferred not to have an open coffin.

'No incense', he had requested. So we lit a few candles smelling of honey.

> **'The night before his coffin was driven round Ulverston on a flat bed truck. We visited his works and a couple of pubs'**

The night before the committal his coffin was driven round Ulverston on a flat bed truck. We visited his works and a couple of pubs accompanied by a wild percussion band, with salsa brass and firecrackers; then returned to the house.

We knew he preferred cremation so we negotiated with the crematorium manager for a double slot at the beginning of the day to gain time to decorate the space and take it all down afterwards. We hung the crem' with simple big banners in blue and red suspended from theatrical lighting stands and put marigolds and sunflowers in earthenware vases. We framed it all with strings of small white papercuts cut with fire and bird imagery and made it more cosy with pools of warm lighting. Incidentally, we did have to remove temporarily a crucifix and cover up a statue depicting a sentimental Jesus story about the sheep that escaped.

'The white seed decorations, painted on the top of the coffin resembled galaxies'

Rather unconventionally, we arranged the seats in a circle and placed the coffin on trestles in the middle. On the floor was a bright red Persian carpet (which we borrowed from a shop in town). It looked fantastic. The white seed decorations, painted on the top of the coffin resembled galaxies and the surrounding banners gave the feeling of a womb-like tent.

The service was a bit longer than usual because many people wanted to read poems and tell stories. We gave out photocopied sheets of some of his poems and later made a few handmade books as presents for those who had helped.

The music was great. His son, a musical director, arranged a few tunes for cellos, trombone and trumpet with a small acapella choir who helped us sing along. "What is the Life of a Man" was hung up on a song sheet! Bryan always said he wanted a song sheet at his funeral because no one ever knows the words of the hymns, but really because he was theatrical and loved pantomimes. Painting the words and hanging the banner took so long we nearly had to abandon the idea but it was worth it ...

Funeral rituals inspired by the Maoris

Dr Jean Hera is an 'ecofeminist' closely working with the Palmerston North Women's Homedeath Support Group in New Zealand, helping to organise funerals without funeral directors – the group was highly commended in the 1994 Social Innovations Awards (see Re-Inventing Society, Institute for Social Inventions, *1994, page 245). Her 376-page PhD thesis,* Reclaiming the Last Rites (Rights) –Women and After-death policy, practices and beliefs in Aotearoa/New Zealand, *draws inspiration from the community-based, often matriarchal, death rites of the Maori peoples, so as to suggest an alternative approach to what she sees as the patriarchal, institutionalised and environmentally hostile approach currently dominant. In the following extracts, Hera uses interviews with women to suggest some of the ways in which the open emotion and informality of Maori death rites could provide a more therapeutic alternative to conventional, European-style funerals.*

Karen spoke of the importance of the honest sharing at the *tangi* (Maori funeral rites) and how this can involve humour:

Creative Endings, £5·95 by credit card from The Natural Death Centre, tel London 0181 208 2853

You bloody bitch, what about that fifty dollars you still owe me? ... I'll never get that now ... You better have it when I get to see you, when I get up there.

Patricia expressed the importance of honestly releasing her feelings of anger at her father's suicide and how she was given the opportunity to do this at his *tangi*:

I can remember the night we buried him ... I was so angry I screamed and yelled and shook the sides of the coffin. I shook the coffin so really hard ...Nobody hassled me or said don't do this ... they just let me go ... and it was good.

Mere talked about the open expression of grief at the *tangi* over a number of days and the therapeutic value of this:

'Join the lines of the dead to the dead and join the lines of the living to the living'

I've always loved what they say at the finish ... "join the lines of the dead to the dead and join the lines of the living to the living and you've done your grieving and now you must pick up life again" ... the family has got no more tears left often by the time the period's finished and they can start picking up the pieces.

Dr Jean Hera, Palmerston North Women's Homedeath Support Group, PO Box 4253, Palmerston North, New Zealand (tel 06 3587139).

Funeral balloons threaten turtles

Ann Hunt

From a letter to the Institute

I am all in favour of 'Green' funerals. However, I feel I must take issue with what I (and many others) feel would be a tragedy as far as our environment is concerned. This is the use of a balloon release as part of a funeral.

'Turtles tend to confuse balloons with jellyfish, eat them, and die'

With regard to the marine environment in particular, balloons are a disaster. Turtles, for example, tend to confuse them with jellyfish, eat them, and die as a result. They can also contribute towards the problem of litter generally, both on land and in our seas. So it hardly seems to be very 'Green' to release them in the first place. The fact that the materials from which balloons can be made these days break down more readily is not really much of an answer – the damage could well

be done before that happened. It is too great a risk to take if we wish to protect our environment.
Ann Hunt, Danegeld, Walford, Ross-on-Wye, Herefordshire HR9 5SA.

Tribal funeral practices around the world

Dancing on the grave – encounters with death *by Nigel Barley (published by John Murray, 1995, ISBN 0 7195 5286 9, hardback, 240 pages, £19-99). Reviewed by Nicholas Albery.*

As one would expect from the author of the riotously funny book *The Innocent Anthropologist*, Nigel Barley's book on death and dying, *Dancing on the grave*, is a witty string of amazing anecdotes.

'Recognise that our ingrained habits are not given by nature'

I regret that Barley refuses to make recommendations for our culture based on his survey of practices around the world – "there are no simple solutions to our own problems to be derived, off-the-peg, from the usages of others. No ready-made ceremonial or image will make death immediately 'all right'; and turn its sting into a kiss." The only lesson we can learn, he says, from the enormous variety of ways of dealing with death in different cultures, is to recognise that our ingrained habits are not given by nature and are therefore not necessarily immutable.

He is somewhat scornful of 'bereavement counsellors' – "it is not surprising that a culture where disposal of the dead has been entirely taken over by paid professionals should make grief management the next marketable skill." But he also pokes fun at the 'd-i-y' natural burial movement for trying to get away from paid professionals:

'd-i-y, making your own coffin, interring it in the garden, is like the budgie laid to rest in a cigar box writ large'

"The stress on d-i-y, making your own coffin, interring it in the garden with a bit of poetry, is like the budgie laid to rest in a cigar box writ large ... The concern of d-i-y activists with the wrapping of the body – no hardwood coffins, biodegradable fittings, recycled paper containers – echoes exactly their protests at the unnecessary wrappings of fish fingers." For us to be devoured by plants and trees is, he adds, "all very well – even poetic – by animals unpleasant. Thus, in a sense, we all die vegetarian deaths".

Creative Endings, £5-95 by credit card from The Natural Death Centre, tel London 0181 208 2853

But mostly Barley swoops around the world, like a vulture picking up juicy titbits. You may care to share the tasting of his feast that follows – but do not be disgusted, rather agree with Montaigne that "Each man calls barbarism whatever is not his own practice". As to why each of the practices is thought to have evolved, you will have to read Barley's astonishing book.

- For Australian Warramungas, the etiquette of mourning requires the men to gash their thighs with deep wounds;
- Amongst the Bwende of Central Africa, the obligation to cry may last so long that women have been known to go blind from the constant weeping;
- The Betsileo of Madagascar mark a funeral with orgiastic and incestuous sex;
- The Dogon of Mali, once they have performed funerary rituals for an absent man, will refuse to recognise him if he happens to return alive.
- The Javanase are said to show a lack of hysteria about corpses due to a belief that the dead provide the living with a lesson in unengaged aloofness.
- The Merina in Madagascar take the bodies out of the tombs to dance and talk with them, and to show them recent changes in the area before returning them to their tombs.
- A mixed Buddhist-Taoist religion in China used to preserve celebrated priests, sometimes by lacquering the body with gold. The priests would be expected to co-operate in reducing the amount of work required, by fasting before death so as to dry out the body.
- The Mbuti pygmies in Africa refuse to recall the dead, and their names are forbidden to be spoken.
- For the Jivaro, the rotting of the body allows re-use by the living of the dead person's face, identity and name.
- Dogon widowers of women who have died in childbirth have to have sex with a stranger in order to be cleansed, even if they have to resort to rape.
- In the Lower Congo, the body of a Bwende VIP would be turned and smoked over a slow fire. Once dry, perhaps a year later, it would be wrapped in mats and cloths, creating a figure three times its original size, then buried standing upright, with, underneath it, several slaves pinned down in the tomb and buried alive.
- The Nuba of Southern Sudan practise circumcision exclusively on the dead.
- Among the Karo Batak of Sumatra, it is said that a banana would be inserted in a dead girl's vagina and a dead boy's penis would be wrapped in warm bamboo.

> **'In Ancient Rome, it was considered wicked to execute a virgin. The ethical problem was solved by having her raped by the jailer'**

- In West Africa, an Asante woman who dies in childbirth is insulted by all the women of the village and dumped on the rubbish heap.
- In Ancient Rome, it was apparently considered wicked to execute a virgin. The ethical problem was solved by having her raped by the jailer.

- In some developing countries, death from old age is so rare that cultures will deny natural death entirely, with almost all deaths attributed to witchcraft and sorcery.

> **'His ashes are to be mixed with breadcrumbs and scattered on the steps of the National Gallery, there to be reprocessed by pigeons as action painting'**

Finally, I enjoyed the plans of a London art critic for the disposal of his remains – his ashes are to be "mixed with breadcrumbs and scattered on the steps of the National Gallery, there to be reprocessed by pigeons as 'action painting' that will communicate his views on such art to the Gallery's trustees".

The Celebration Box

The following is an adapted extract from an article in Country Living (June '96) by Fraser Harrison.

Yvonne Malik is an honorary consultant of the Natural Death Centre and is listed in its literature as a coffin decorator, but when I went to see her in her cottage in Wray in the Lune valley, near Lancaster, she was keener to talk about her concept of the 'Celebration Box'. She showed me an example that had been put together using an old house-painter's box, a stout wooden case with a large metal handle and shallow, interlocking shelves.

> **'Every part of the box overflowed with photographs, keepsakes and small items'**

It was dedicated to Lilian and Horace Parker and was filled with mementos of them, his on one side, hers on the other. Every part of the box overflowed with photographs, keepsakes and small items connected with the couple, from the jaunty cigarette holder of Horace's youth to a minute, beaded evening bag belonging to Lilian.

Thanks to the skill with which this miniature museum had been assembled, its bits and pieces radiated a surprising vitality, forming an unusual object that was both an obituary and a memorial. Yvonne says that the function of the celebration box (she intends to design a simpler version for sale) is to help people who are more at ease with non-verbal means of communicating.

"Filling something like a Celebration Box can be a shared family experience and a way of remembering. It is portable and easily accessible, and something we can do for ourselves, which will also be of later comfort to the bereaved." Despite her preoccupation with the funereal – she has already ordered her own coffin which she plans to decorate – Yvonne is good-humoured and far from morbid. She simply wants to assist those who have been prompted by loss, age, illness or, as in her case, a philosophical temperament, to make ready for death on their own terms.

A Celebration Box at the back of the church
Yvonne Malik

Here is an adapted extract from Yvonne Malik's leaflet about the Celebration Box:

When a relative or close friend dies, we often find it impossible to find words to express our feelings. We remember special times, events and places which we shared together, or recall good deeds and kindnesses. These keys to our special memories have an intrinsic value only between ourselves and the one who has died.

Using the Celebration Box is an opportunity to express and focus on a new way of saying 'goodbye'. Each box becomes unique and special, giving us the satisfaction of having taken part in filling it, as well as the ultimate feeling of something shared. This is a new way of including family and friends in a non-verbal act of celebration and comfort – a celebration of the life and shared experiences with the deceased and a later comfort for the bereaved, as well as something to be treasured by the next generation.

Suggested items which have a private or intimate meaning and could be placed in the box include:

Photographs; postcards which reminds us of a special day together; letters, poems, thank-you notes; birthday cards; ticket from a concert which we shared, souvenir from a holiday; button from their favourite jacket, pair of earrings, pipe; copy of a team certificate, club badge, medal; special scarf or cap.

The events and times which we shared require no explanation from us and the tokens placed within the box are private statements. It is something which can be carried out by ourselves, alongside the traditional services of the funeral director.

'The Celebration Box can be filled at home prior to the funeral or placed in an accessible situation at the back of the church'

The Celebration Box can be filled at home prior to the funeral or placed in an accessible situation at the back of the church or chapel and brought home after the final ceremony.

Each Celebration Box is hand decorated and therefore differs from any other. It also has the advantage of being portable, to suit today's more transient lifestyle.

I have also worked out a flat pack design whereby it could be mass produced – on strong card which can be printed flat then folded.

If you might like to commission an individual Celebration Box, or to discuss helping to produce them in larger quantities, please contact Yvonne Malik, Sweet Briar Cottage, 52 Hornby Road, Wray, Lancashire LA2 8QN (tel 015242 21767).

A tombstone with flat-screen video
Joey Shamel

From The Point (March '96; published by the First Millennial Foundation, Pasadena Chapter, 235 E. Colorado Blvd., No. 371 Pasadena, CA 91101, USA).

Mara Gendel of Long Beach, California, has designed a 'Tombstone of Tomorrow'. She proposes a gravestone with a flat display screen on it. People visiting could just reach out and activate a prerecorded message from the deceased person. It could be a spoken message or scenes the person wanted to be remembered by.

Her idea won her the Great Idea Contest in the February '96 issue of Popular Science, a contest for young people, aged 8 to 16, who had come up with new inventions.

Neo-classical ceramic memorial urns

Adapted from information sent to the Natural Death Centre.

Rupert Blamire, who has a masters degree in ceramics from the Royal College of Art, has designed a striking neo-classical three-foot-high lidded ceramic urn, made of red terracotta clay from Staffordshire. They can be used for housing the ashes or simply be used as garden ornaments – indeed they won the 1994 Garden Product of the Year award from the BBC's Gardener's World Live show.

Rupert Blamire, Ground Floor Unit, Bannerman Buildings, Bannerman Road, Bristol BS5 ORR (tel 0117 939 3914). The three-foot urn costs £95, the four-foot urn costs £325. Blamire will deliver for about £40 (within the region).

Distributing ashes to Poste Restantes
Anthony Judge

From an e-mail to the Institute.

For those who are dissatisfied with burial and possibilities for placing burial urns after cremation, there are other possibilities.

The suggestion is to provide oneself with a mailing list of Poste Restante addresses in isolated locations in different countries around the world. Getting the addresses together is merely a question of using an atlas and looking for small towns or villages in isolated locations – possibly with marvellous topography, just where one would like the ashes of loved ones to rest. Make the address on an envelope: Poste Restante, Name of Town. A hundred so addressed envelopes could be made in this way.

'Put a few ashes in each envelope, seal it, and send them off to Poste Restantes'

Following the cremation, all that remains is to put a few ashes in each envelope, seal it, and send them off.

What then happens is that the envelope arrives at the Poste Restante office in each location and stays there for some months. It is then treated as waste paper and either burnt or dumped. In this way a person gets their ashes distributed around the world for the price of a small mailing.

Of course, a more elegant arrangement would be to reach international agreement on the treatment of such envelopes. They could be opened and the ashes scattered at the local burial ground. But this is for the future.

Anthony Judge, Union of International Associations, Rue Washington 40, B-1050 Brussels, Belgium (tel 32 2 640 18 08; fax 32 2 646 0525; e-mail: <uia@uia.be>; WWW Home Page: <http://www.uia.org/>).

Make your own video message memorial

From an announcement put out by the Natural Death Centre.

Thom Osborn, a British filmmaker, is offering a service to help people record a video of themselves, to be played after their death.

'Four people bravely recorded their messages for posterity in front of an audience'

The service, called 'Video Message Memorials', was successfully tried out at the English Day of the Dead event on April 21st '96, at which four people bravely recorded their messages for posterity in front of an audience.

Such a message could be laid down at any time of life, and for a variety of posthumous purposes. The video might perhaps be shown at one's funeral, or contain a particular message for a loved one or for future generations, or contain advice to children.

"Whatever your impulse," says Osborn, "whoever you are speaking to, I will film it for you (and help you to formulate what you want to say, if you wish)."

The normal cost would be £40 for one hour (£30 for any subsequent hour), the price to include making a copy onto VHS tape. Concessionary rates are available by negotiation. Thom Osborn, 1 Brecknock Road, London N7 OBL (tel 0171 482 0600).

Obituaries for the ordinary

Obits – The way we say goodbye *by MaryEllen Gillan (published by Serious Publishing, 7249 Waverley Avenue, Burnaby, BC V5 4A7, Canada (tel 001 604 879 0321; fax 001 604 875 0007). Reviewed by Nicholas Albery.*

I am a believer in the idea that anyone, however so-called 'ordinary', is entitled to an obituary, especially now that cyberspace 'immortality', an obituary on the Web, should rapidly descend in price. I therefore welcome this book, *Obits*, which collects obituaries of 'ordinary' Canadians. They are admittedly a trifle dull, many of them. But it's a start, and I like the way the author encourages people to write more memorable obituaries and to send them in to her.

'Obituarist for the masses – out of work novelists'

Perhaps many people need assistance from yet another professional: the obituarist for the masses – out of work novelists, or the officiant or priest who conducted the funeral, earning an extra bob or two on the side.

It may be though, once obituaries start transferring to the Web en masse, that there will be an unleashing of creativity as obituaries go multimedia and free form.

Memorial services for the living

Adapted extracts from an item entitled 'Early Call' in The Guardian (Nov 8th '95) monitored for the Institute by Yvonne Malik.

Friends of a ninety-two-year-old Tewkesbury church warden invited him to his own memorial service as a way of celebrating his life.

Making love in the afterlife

Adapted extract from Bright Air, Brilliant Fire *by Gerald Edelman.*

A dying man consoles his grieving wife that he will return six weeks after his death. If she visits a Medium, she will meet him again. After his death, the wife waits six weeks and visits a Medium. Sure enough, she hears her husband's voice –
"Hello Darling."

Creative Endings, £5·95 by credit card from The Natural Death Centre, tel London 0181 208 2853

"Harry, is that you?"
"Yes, it's me."
"What do you do all day?"
The voice replies:

> 'I get up, make love, walk, make love, eat, make love, sleep, make love – and the next day the same'

"I get up, make love, walk, make love, eat, make love, sleep, make love – and the next day the same."
"But darling, I didn't know angels in heaven made love."
The voice replied:
"I'm not an angel in heaven, I'm a rabbit in Saskatchewan."

Virtual immortality for everyone alive today

Professor John Wren-Lewis

Before and After *(page 46, published by the Natural Death Centre, 1995) carried a short feature about the book* The Physics of Immortality – Modern Cosmology, God and the Resurrection of the Dead *by Frank Tipler (published by Macmillan, 1994, $39.95). Here is a longer review, an adapted extract from an essay entitled 'By computer and spacecraft to God and eternity', sent to the Natural Death Centre by John Wren-Lewis.*

If you want to know what a real 'new paradigm' scientific world-view might look like, as contrasted with the old-hat pseudo-scientific world-views which often currently sail under the 'new paradigm' flag, read this book *The Physics of Immortality* by the professor of physics at Tulane University in New Orleans.

Having recently spent months struggling to find an arresting opening for my own book (I think with some success), this one leaves mine for dead:

> 'Physics will permit the resurrection to eternal life of everyone who has ever lived'

"This book is a description of the Omega Theory," it begins, "which is a *testable* physical theory for an omnipresent, omniscient and omnipotent God who will ... resurrect every single one of us to live forever in an abode which is in all essentials the Judeo-Christian Heaven ... I shall make no appeal, anywhere, to revelation. I shall appeal only to the solid results of modern physical science ... I shall show *exactly* how physics will permit the resurrection to eternal life of everyone who has ever lived, is living, or will live. I shall show *exactly* why this power to resurrect, which modern physics allows, ...*will in fact be used.*" (The italics are mine, but Tipler is completely serious about all these claims, and gives detailed calculations to back them up.)

Tipler, the self-styled unrepentant reductionist, speaks like a true mystic who knows there is more to matter than evolution has yet uncovered – but true to his scientific brief, he makes no appeal to magic or the supernatural. He appeals to what science and technology are already uncovering right here in our present earthly back yard about the potential of matter to support intelligence in non-organic forms, in machines such as the one on which I am writing this review right now.

'To transfer our whole minds inside computers weighing 100+ grams each'

Tipler (who goes well beyond PhD level in Computer Complexity Theory) gives ground for thinking that, well before the end of the next century, we shall have been able to transfer our whole minds *with the full sensuous enjoyment-capacity and feeling-capacity of our biological inheritance* inside self-replicating nanotechnological computers weighing more than 100 grams each – and since they need experience no time-lapse while travelling, colonising the entire galaxy with (or rather as) them will be a piece of cake. With that much ecological space to play with (to say nothing of the fact that energy requirements of individual personal existence in that form are minimal), there is no question of scarcity, which, Tipler argues (again drawing on some pretty formidable authorities) is the root of all so-called evil impulses.

'Gravity-shear, the power to stop the contraction of the universe'

Colonising the rest of the universe will take a little longer – several million million years, in fact – but Tipler argues that because the most basic of all life-drives at the root of consciousness is survival, colonisation will surely happen, well before the point where the expansion of the universe goes into reverse towards the 'big crunch'. And at that stage, the vastly expanded collective intelligence of the colonised universe – the Omega consciousness – will have at Its disposal the unimaginable energy of gravity-shear, which will give It the power to stop the contraction and create a stable cosmic paradise of truly eternal finite life.

Tipler establishes, by appeal to game theory, that Omega consciousness must of Its very nature be utterly generous towards every sentient life-form that has contributed to Its own vast evolutionary struggle – so It will have both the power

Creative Endings, £5-95 by credit card from The Natural Death Centre, tel London 0181 208 2853

and the imperative to resurrect all who have ever lived, good and bad alike, into Its own blissful time-transcendence. And in that condition, there will be absolutely no problems of overcrowding or denial of space for individuality, nor any pressure on time for doing whatever each one wants to do – and therefore neither unfreedom nor boredom.

'Using advanced versions of techniques already known in a computer theory for "fleshing out" imperfectly-recalled data'

For the ultimate resurrection, Tipler argues in great detail that personal identity can be exactly reconstructed by progressive 'unpacking' of memory-data back through history, using advanced versions of techniques already known in a computer theory for 'fleshing out' imperfectly-recalled data – a deliberate employment of the processes that already happen when genes produce bodies and brains produce the memories that make up 'experience'.

At first sight, it's something of a puzzle that his book hasn't gone off like a bomb in spiritual and religious circles, considering the popularity of other books linking modern science with spiritual issues, like Capra's *The Tao of Physics*. True, there are many points where Tipler overestimates the general reader's capacity for grasping even simple ideas in relativistic cosmology; even I, who did the subject for my degree, am still quite unable to say whether his assertions about the Bekenstein Bound or the Higgs Boson make sense or not. But that kind of difficulty applied equally to Capra's book, and even more to Stephen Hawking's *A Brief History of Time*, which had a far more negative conclusion that Tipler's, yet became a best-seller. So why is Tipler's book still only trickling off the shelves?

'The urge for personal significance is as fundamental to human consciousness as the urge for survival'

I think he puts his finger on the answer in the very last sentence of his main text, when he asserts that "Religion is now a part of science". This is implied by his whole argument, and I think he just does not realise that the psychological effect is to leave the great majority feeling 'left out', because it means there is no *significant* contribution they can make to humanity's 'salvation'. Since being born again as a mystic, I've come to recognise that the urge for personal significance is as fundamental to human consciousness as the urge for survival, and not to be dismissed as mere 'ego'. So I can quite see that it's not just clergy who might be less than wildly enthusiastic about Tipler's book, because it could make them redundant; he may not intend his Omega Point to seem too distant from our lives to matter, but that's how it come across, if the evolution leading up to it, from here

'Our undeniably spectacular home planet, necessarily perishable in the long term, could be resurrected to share God's eternity'

But do read it, all the same, for even if his peers eventually declare his conclusions doubtful or invalid, it's still very important indeed in showing how even the most reductionist science today implies the spiritual perspective. And it should force us all to think again about whether current 'green' attempts to curb scientific and technological advances in the name of love for Planet Earth may not in fact be theologically short-sighted underestimates of humanity's spiritual destiny, which, according to both St Paul and Tipler, may be to the only means whereby our undeniably spectacular home planet, necessarily perishable in the long term on current world-views (and maybe the not-so-long term, if that wandering asteroid hits), could be resurrected to share God's eternity.

Professor John Wren-Lewis, 1/22 Cliffbrook Parade, Clovelly, NSW 2031, Australia. John Wren-Lewis's book about his own continuing mystical experience (induced by eating a poisoned sweet in Thailand) – The 9.15 to Nirvana – *is due to be published before the end of 1996.*

LETTERS

Canal boat cruises during terminal illness

James B. Marshall

Adapted extracts from an appeal sent to the Natural Death Centre.

I am seeking investments in multiples of £500 towards the £22,000 still needed to begin my project of buying and fitting out a narrowboat, so that any terminally ill person (plus four family or friends) can cruise on the Bath end of the Kennet and Avon Canal. I have £10,000 to put into this. Your investments would be tied to the value of the boat and would tend to rise in value.

One thing I have found is that those who are terminally ill, and their family and friends, want to spend a few memorable days together. I have distilled the details of this project from 35 years of experience on canals and rivers.

James B. Marshall, Collhaven, 17 Fore Street, Bishopsteignton, South Devon TQ14 9QR (tel & fax 01626 775511).

Messages written on papier maché coffins
Pamela Gray

Adapted extract from a letter to the Natural Death Centre from Australia.

I have set up a very small paper recycling business in the village I live in, South of Sydney. This has led me to an interest in making beautiful and environmentally-sound coffins from waste paper (and in promoting healthier deaths for those that want them).

A neighbour got some information about your Natural Death Centre from the Internet for me.

> 'Everyone could write messages on the coffin, like they do on plaster over broken bones'

I like the idea of the coffin being a functional, everyday item, like a bookcase, coffee table or blanket box. If I can do papier maché coffins, and stay within Australian health regulations, people could decorate or put the final touches onto their coffin, or everyone could write messages, like they do on plaster over broken bones. Or have pages from their favourite magazine or their life issue articles plastered all over the coffin.

Pamela Gray, PO Box 188, Milton NSW 2538, Australia.

Centre for Living and Dying in the States
Cliff Aguirre

From an e-mail to the Natural Death Centre.

I am one of the organisers of an organisation called The Center for Living and Dying, MA. Our organisation has three main goals:

- To change society's view on death from an experience to be feared to an experience to be at peace with.
- To help the dying to die in peace without fear and to allow them to understand that at death, they continue. That death is just the discarding of the physical vehicle. That you live on as the eternal being which you have always been.
- To help the families of the dying to understand that death is not an end but a transition and that they will see their loved one again. We help with their bereavement.

Our organisers range from people who work with cancer patients, to workers in hospices and a writer on a book called *The Death Transition*.

We would like to know if we could have our Web Page linked to your Natural Death Centre. Our URL is <http://www.xensei.com/users/aci>.

Cliff Aguirre (e-mail: <aci@xensei.com>).

Practising for dying
Thom Osborn

From a notice sent to the Natural Death Centre.

Do you think regularly about your mortality, as a way of getting friendly with dying?

I am planning a documentary film about practising – of different kinds – told through the practice and words of four people engaged in an activity that is important to them.

I'm looking for someone who meditates on death, as one of these four. If you might be interested and would like to know more., please contact me.

Thom Osborn, 1a Brecknock Road, London N7 OBL (tel 0171 482 0600).

Seeing and touching the dead body
Stephen Briggs

From a letter to the Natural Death Centre.

Thank you for the *Natural Death Handbook* which I have spent the day absorbed in. It is excellent! Since coming across Elizabeth Kubler-Ross's work in the mid seventies, I have been interested in a more personally responsible approach to dying, and, in my work as a Jungian therapist, the issues of the 'soul' are ever before me. I value your book for its wealth of real information, warmth and humane cheer.

> 'The phrase "viewing the body" is coldly impersonal'

A turn of phrase is oft repeated in the book which I am left wondering about and, though it belongs to the standard vocabulary of death, seems to me oddly out of place in this book. It is the phrase "viewing the body". I know this to be what one does and what one asks to do. But I wonder why we only use that word "view". It is coldly impersonal and conveys a sense of distance and slight distaste. It perpetuates the 'keep at a distance and do not touch' inclination, which runs against the mother's instinct so movingly illustrated in one of the stories in the book. To "see" the body, or "look at the body" imply more interest than is culturally normal and is a bit too explicit perhaps, but for me is nearer to what we are keen to improve.

'As a cabinet maker, I would be glad to assist now and then with the occasional coffin'

An absorbing interest in cabinet making lasting many years has enabled me to furnish a respectable workshop of woodworking tools and the occasional coffin would not be difficult for me to supply to suit the pocket of any needy enquirer who might want for encouragement in organising their own funeral. I would be glad to assist now and then within the constraints of a very busy life, so I am willing to help if you know of any who are particularly stuck.

Stephen Briggs, 42 Vanbrugh Park, London SE3 7AA (tel 0181 293 3365).

Editorial comment

Perhaps "visiting the body" might be better than "seeing" or "looking at", since visiting could include touch.

A recognised sign to indicate bereavement

Adapted extracts from a letter from Fran Duncan to the Natural Death Centre.

Could today's society benefit from the reintroduction of a recognised sign indicating a person was going through a bereavement process?

'Should I keep up the bright conversational tone, or should I mention my dad's passing?'

One day I was walking along the High Street, and met an acquaintance with a newly-born child in a push chair. She asked how I was, and I wondered what to say? Should I keep up the bright conversational tone, or should I mention my dad's passing? It was four months since he had died, so would it be considered 'valid' to bring the subject up?

In the end I did mention it. It turned out that she had also recently lost a parent, so we had useful experiences to exchange.

A black armband (or modern equivalent, such as a symbol of a heart with a tear dropping from it), by 'telling my story for me', would have avoided my dilemma.

Fran Duncan, 8 Blankney Close, Guisborough, Cleveland TS14 7PA.

Publications available

This form can be photocopied or orders can be placed by phone (with credit card and with a small supplementary charge) or by letter (with cheque from a UK-based bank in £s sterling).

• I wish to be sent the following ticked PUBLICATIONS – (P & p included. 10% off for Institute subscribers, except for those books marked [*])

[*] **'The Natural Death Handbook'**, cheap, Green and DIY funerals, Good Funeral Guide to undertakers, caring for the dying at home, preparing for dying, living wills, alternatives to euthanasia, Near-Death Experiences, manifesto. £10-95. Or from Natural Death Centre direct.

[*] **'Green Burial – the d-i-y guide to law and practice'**, book re burial on own land etc, £9-85, 2nd edition. Or from Natural Death Centre direct.

[*] **'Information pack'** on Natural Death Centre, funerals, green burial grounds, cardboard coffins by mail, etc. Six first class stamps or £1-56 (free with both above books).

[*] **'Death Plan'**, **'Advance Funeral Wishes'** and **'Living Will'** forms, sensible preparations for dying. £1-04 or four first class stamps.

[*] **'Before and After – The best new ideas for improving the quality of dying and for inexpensive, green, family-organised funerals'**, £5-95, 1995. Or from Natural Death Centre direct.

[*] **'Creative Endings'**, creative ways of approaching dying and funerals, £5-95, 1996. Or from Natural Death Centre direct.

[*] **'Poem for the Day – 366 Poems, Old and New, Worth Learning By Heart'**, with foreword by Wendy Cope. 400 page book with a poem for each day of the year and prizes for learning them. £11-49. Or from Natural Death Centre direct.

• **'DIY Futures'**, 250 new social tools and incentives, £14-85, 1996.
• **'Best Ideas – A compendium of social innovations'**, £14-85, 1995.
• **'Social Innovations – A compendium'**, £9-85, 1994.
• **'The Book of Visions, An Encyclopedia of Social Innovations'**, foreword by Anita Roddick; a 352 A4 page compendium of best ideas and projects. £18-49 (£20-65 from abroad by credit card) incl. p&p.
• **'The Forest Garden'** by Robert Hart. How to establish a Forest Garden, in town or country, consisting entirely of fruit and nut trees and bushes, wild and self-seeding vegetables and herbs; £3-25. 3rd edition.
• **'Alternative Gomera** – Guide to a fortnight's walking round Gomera Island near Tenerife' by Nicholas Albery, 2nd Edition, £6-50. Map £4-95 extra.
• **'Re-Inventing Democracy'**. Designs for more responsive, yet more stable, governance by David Chapman, advance price £8-95 (£13-95 libraries & institutions). To be published '97 or '98
• **'The Neal's Yard Story'**, full of useful ideas for small businesses and urban renewal. £1-95.
• **'How to Save the World'**, by John Seymour, Ivan Illich, Robert Jungk, Theodore Roszak and others. £4-95, 319 pages.
• The book **'Community Counselling Circles'** by John Southgate, for improving the atmosphere in groups. £6-95; libraries etc. £9-95.

Creative Endings, £5-95 by credit card from The Natural Death Centre, tel London 0181 208 2853

78 Creative Endings

- 'The Solution for South Africa', an influential cantonisation scheme, as a way of avoiding the coming civil war in South Africa. £7.
- 'Social Invention Workshops – A Manual for Use in Schools', used by the Institute in its school workshops. £2-50.
- 'Future Workshops – How to Create Desirable Futures', by Robert Jungk, used by groups throughout Europe as a manual. £8-85.
- 'The Problem Solving Pocketbook', an overview of all the main ways to solve problems, plus some wild ones. £2-95.
- 'Opening the Mind's Eye', by Margaret Chisman. Group exercises on themes such as truth, beauty and goodness, designing new commandments, etc. £2-50.
- 'Being True to Yourself', by Margaret Chisman, completes her trilogy of exercises for groups. These ones encourage insight and self-understanding. £4-95.
- **LOGO for Windows**. Fun software plus game for learning maths and programming. £25 (software item).
- 'Learning Computer Programming in One Day – A Guide to BBC Basic'. £2-95. By an 11 year old for novices.
- 'Auction of Promises – how to raise £16,000 in one evening', by Kara Conti, for church, school and community groups. How to auction off services such as 4 hours' massage, computer consultancy etc £1-95.
- 'The Book of Oaths – A Compendium of Ethical Codes for Scientists'. £3-50.
- The Institute **Journal**, old back issues £3 each, £10 for a random five back issues.

- Enclosed is £15 for an Institute **subscription**. Pay by UK Standing Order if possible, in which case £1 off: £14. (Outside UK £17 by credit card)

- (Alternatively and at no extra charge) I wish to apply for **membership**, and enclose £15 (outside UK £17 by credit card) and details of profession, skills and interests, and of socially innovative projects or ideas. (Please also enclose a 70 word summary of these details for the 'Who's Who Directory of Social Inventors').

(£1 off above £15 fee for those who pay by UK banker's order – fill in form below. Members and subscribers receive the annual book-length Annual in the summer – *state if you want this year's or next year's* – a regionalised Who's Who booklet, and 10% off most Institute publications, except those with [*]. They can also apply to join walks near London most Saturdays and Salon discussions.)

- I also wish to make a **donation** and enclose £...... / I am prepared to offer services as a volunteer / or to send socially inventive cuttings from enclosed list of publications.
- I enclose a card (and address) of **friend** to whom these goods are to be sent.

Outside UK:
- 10% extra for sea-mail postage, 50% extra if wanting airmail on books.

Outside UK, unless paying by credit card or by UK cheque or UK cash notes, you must add:
- £3-50 (if paying by foreign or Irish cash notes, for bank charges)
- £10 (if paying by foreign cheque – even from Eire – for bank charges)
- No extra if paying UK sterling by bankers draft **with bank charges paid your end**: (to Institute for Social Inventions account, bank number 60 13 34, account number

---

Creative Endings, £5-95 by credit card from The Natural Death Centre, tel London 0181 208 2853

38843803, bank address: National Westminster Bank, 298 Elgin Avenue, London W9, UK).

Payment by credit card: please add 4.2% for the bank's fee, unless otherwise stated. We accept any non-Switch card with American Express, Access, Eurocard, Mastercard or Visa logos. by phone, fax or letter, give your card-holder number, expiry date, registered address, name and initials & signature. This is the cheapest way to pay from outside UK.

NAME (caps) ....

ADDRESS...

....

....

TEL. No. ....

Please return this form with cheques payable to: '**Institute for Social Inventions**', 20 Heber Road, London NW2 6AA, (tel 0181 208 2853; fax 0181 452 6434; e-mail: <rhino@dial.pipex.com>).

■■■■■■■■■■■■■■■■■■■■■■■■■

UK STANDING ORDER FORM – please fill in and return to Institute for Social Inventions, 20 Heber Road, London NW2 6AA. USE CAPITALS.

MY BANK...

BANK ADDRESS..

....

MY ACCOUNT NO. ....

Please pay to the Institute for Social Inventions £....... **annually**, starting on the ...... day of .... 19....... (or as soon after this date as possible). Their account is bank number 60 13 34, account number 38843803, bank address: National Westminster Bank, 298 Elgin Avenue, London W9, UK.

NAME (caps) ....

ADDRESS...

....

TEL. No. ....

SIGNATURE...

DATE...

Creative Endings, £5-95 by credit card from The Natural Death Centre, tel London 0181 208 2853